The Gift of Silence

The Gift of Silence

And Other Considerations for
Effective Communications

Rob Scanlon

Copyright © 2022 by Rob Scanlon.

Library of Congress Control Number: 2022916208
ISBN: Hardcover 978-1-6698-4541-6
Softcover 978-1-6698-4540-9
eBook 978-1-6698-4542-3

All rights reserved. No part of this book may be reproduced or transmitted in any form or by any means, electronic or mechanical, including photocopying, recording, or by any information storage and retrieval system, without permission in writing from the copyright owner.

Any people depicted in stock imagery provided by Getty Images are models, and such images are being used for illustrative purposes only. Certain stock imagery © Getty Images.

Print information available on the last page.

Rev. date: 09/09/2022

To order additional copies of this book, contact:
Xlibris
844-714-8691
www.Xlibris.com
Orders@Xlibris.com
844788

Chapter 1

All the items on her workshop checklist were done.

As it was her habit before every workshop, she took a moment to reflect, to give thanks, to appreciate that her current realities were her past dreams.

She remembered a specific day fifteen years ago, sitting in a diner in Bronxville, New York, with her dad having breakfast, he asked her, "So in terms of your career, where do you want to be in five years or ten years?"

It was a ridiculously ambitious dream at the time, but she wanted to be standing where she was now, helping, teaching other business professionals, and consulting with companies to help them grow.

She picked up her phone. She texted her dad, who was living in Los Angeles, "I love you, Dad. I have another workshop today. Thanks for your encouragement and support. Miss you. Love, Christa." She put her phone in her pocket.

It was 7:57 a.m.

Christa's cell phone vibrated in her pocket. She answered, "Marc, good morning."

Marc sheepishly responded, "Christa, I am sorry to call you so early, but I needed to run something by before a meeting I have this morning. Do you have about five minutes?"

"Absolutely, Marc, I just finished getting everything set up for my workshop at nine. How can I help?"

Marc was an exceptionally competent and experienced senior vice president of sales for a high-flying software company with about fifty sales professionals under his command. "Let me give you a snapshot of the situation. Then I could use your advice." Marc continued, "I have a call with the COO of a health system at eleven. This meeting is to finalize a multimillion-dollar contract—an opportunity we have been working on for fourteen months. The COO was part of our initial conversations, but he has been absent from the process for the last few months. While he has stepped back from the project, this account has been ridiculously and inappropriately demanding. They regularly send complicated requests to our team with four- or six-hour deadlines. They are constantly changing directions on configurations and required features. They are incredibly disrespectful and treat our people like crap. Yesterday, our executive team met and talked about walking away from this account before we sign the contract. The leadership team agreed that we can't put our implementation and service team through this kind of meat grinder because it will seriously hurt our team, hurt our ability to serve other customers, and it will probably be a failure—unhappy customers. Do you have the picture?"

"I think so, Marc."

"Well, given where we are, I have the 'honor' of telling this COO that they need to change things or we are going to part ways. I have the task of getting them to change or firing them before they sign the contract. I put together my talk track for the meeting, I was hoping I could run it by you and get your advice."

"Sure."

Marc read through his talk track. It was quite good. He succinctly listed the specific situations and captured a clear pattern of inconsistent, irrational, and almost abusive behaviors. "So, Christa, your thoughts?"

"It is very good." Then Christa respectfully hesitated.

Marc filled the silence, "I am not wildly off base then?"

"No, not at all. May I ask you a couple questions?"

"Sure."

"Where is the source of the irrational and inappropriate behavior?" Christa probed.

"The VP who manages the project." Marc expanded, "It is pretty much just him. He is out of control."

"Assuming a change in his behavior or role, what are the odds they would be a successful, happy client?"

"Probably very good. They are a very good fit for what we do. This VP is the source of the problem, and everyone else on the health system team seems to take their cues from him."

"Marc, I think what you have is very good. May I put some additional things on the table for you to consider?"

"Please do. That is why I called."

Christa smiled before she spoke. "Let's think about changing the focus or theme of the conversation. If I heard you correctly in your talk track, you said, 'We need to be partners in this project. We are currently not behaving as partners. *We need to change the way we work together.*'" She waited.

"Yes, exactly."

"The implication is, if you can't be partners and work together, then you are walking away." Again, she waited for affirmation.

"Agreed."

"What if we changed the theme to a *great implementation*?" She let the phrase sit for a moment. "We might say something like this to the COO, 'Our goal is for you to be thrilled with us when we are installed and up and running. Therefore, our focus is on a great implementation.' Let that sink in for a moment, and then ask him, Marc, 'How do you think we are tracking right now in terms of having a great implementation?'"

Marc knew where Christa was going with this. "He probably is going to ask me where I think we are in terms of a great implementation. This will create an opening for me to share the details and the pattern, which is very likely to lead to a horrible implementation."

"Correct. A great implementation establishes a shared goal. He is likely to want to hear your thoughts because they relate to what is at stake for him—a great implementation." Christa waited.

"Once I get the problems out on the table in the context of ensuring great implementation, we can, then, go into the specifics of how we work towards being better partners on this journey."

"Great. By changing the focus to great implementation, you will lower the odds that he will see this as a conversation calling one of his children ugly. It improves the odds that he will appreciate your trying to 'watch his back' and to get him to the shared goal of a great implementation."

"Christa, thanks. This is really helpful. I will keep you posted." He paused, then asked, "By the way, where are you? Where is your workshop?"

"Boston."

"Well, have fun. Thank you again. I really appreciate your help."

Christa reviewed her checklist for the second time and then walked down the hall to get a cup of coffee. She was ready and excited for the day ahead.

Chapter 2

The lecture hall was almost filled. There were 150 business professionals registered for the workshop.

It was a lecture hall in a modified *u*-shape, where the rows ascended higher and higher as they moved toward the back of the room.

Christa greeted as many of the participants as she could as they entered the room.

At actually 9:00 a.m., she walked to the center of the room and looked up and across the rows.

"Good morning," she said with a warm smile.

"Good morning." "Good morning." "*Buongiorno,*" the audience responded.

She smiled more widely at the enthusiastic responses and the Italian flavor provided by one of the participants.

"It is a great privilege to be here today and to be your facilitator for our day together."

She let the word *privilege* marinate.

"In preparing for our session today, I tried to put myself in your shoes and think about some of the questions I thought you might have.

"I thought you might want to know

>what are the specific objectives of this workshop?

>What will be the pace of the material? Is this going to be like a leisurely dinner sitting on a canal in Venice, or is it more of a timed hotdog eating contest?

>If I am going to call on any of you and put you on the spot in front of everyone?

>How to get the most out of this workshop?

>How good are the lunches here at Babson?"

She took a couple steps to the right and surveyed the audience. "Are these some of your questions?"

The audience responded with "Yes." "Absolutely." "Yes, especially the lunch question."

She turned her head to the left side of the room. "Any other questions?"

One hand was raised in the fifth row on the left. She acknowledged the hand. The woman asked, "Will we get the slides you are going to use?"

"Thank you for the question." Looking at her tent card, she said, "Yes, Marissa. When we are done at four today, you will all receive an email with a link to Dropbox with the slides."

She waited a moment, then asked, "Any other questions?" There were no other questions. "Great, let me take a few moments to address the questions that were posed.

"First, the lunch here at the Babson Executive Conference Center is fantastic! Save room for dessert! Second, you can relax. We *will* have a dialogue today." Gesturing her hand inclusively out to the audience and back to herself, she continued, "But none of you will be put on the spot. Third, what are we trying to accomplish in this workshop? What are our objectives? To simply state our shared objective: **To leave this room at the end of the day equipped with an arsenal of approaches to make us better communicators.** Does this work for you as an objective?"

The group agreed.

"In terms of the pace of the day, put on your track shoes because we are going move at a very fast pace with *lots* of content. However, I do hope you will find the content tastier and healthier than hotdogs."

She continued to gracefully and comfortably move through all the space at the front of the room and make eye contact with many of the participants.

"As it relates to getting the most out of your investment on this day, I would highly recommend two things:

> First, pick two areas during the day where you have the epiphany of 'I do that. I do what she is talking about.' These areas are likely to be some of your business or

commercial communication strengths. So take note to leverage them often.

Second, pick two areas that hit you right in the middle of the forehead, where you go 'Wow, I need to change that,' or 'Wow, I could really use that.'

"In terms of the rest of material, put it in your quiver for another time. Don't feel burdened that you need to learn to shoot every arrow in the quiver right away."

Almost everyone in the audience was writing a note regarding her counsel. She waited while they recorded their thoughts. She walked over to her laptop to advance her slides to the first section.

When it was clear that everyone had taken a note of how to get the most out of their day together, she advanced to the first slide. It said, *"Why communications?"*

"One of the questions I sometimes get is, 'Christa, why a whole day on business or commercial communications?' This is a fair question."

She paused and walked further up to the front of the room. "If I may"—her tone was inviting—"let me ask you a question. Do you think that over the last fifteen years, we, as a society, have become better or less effective communicators?"

There were many different responses from the audience. "Better." "Faster." "Much worse." "Text-crazy." "Better connected." "Not really connected." "Impersonal." "Terrible listeners." "Shoot and run communicators." "We message." "We don't talk."

The Gift of Silence

She smiled at the passion and the breadth of feedback then asked again, "Do you think that in the last decade or so, we have become more or less self-centered, more or less willing to see things from another's point of view?"

Here, there was unanimity in their feedback. "More selfish." "Less open." "Less respectful."

"Almost all of us have become quite accustomed to communicating all sorts of messages, trivial and tragic, via 140 characters. Today, we live in a world that has never been more divided and more centered on our own individual agendas and own needs. Do we agree?"

She waited for supporting head nods. Surprisingly, there was even a loud "Amen," which brought laughter to the room.

"So if the communication norm today is a snappy 140 characters and the focus is on ourselves, how can this *not* impact communications with our colleagues, with our direct reports, with our clients, and with our prospects?"

The audience agreed.

"We are going to discuss over twenty areas of communication today; thus, the full plate of content and the required track shoes." The large screen held pictures summarizing the communication topics of the day. Each topic had its own image capturing its essence. "These are the topics."

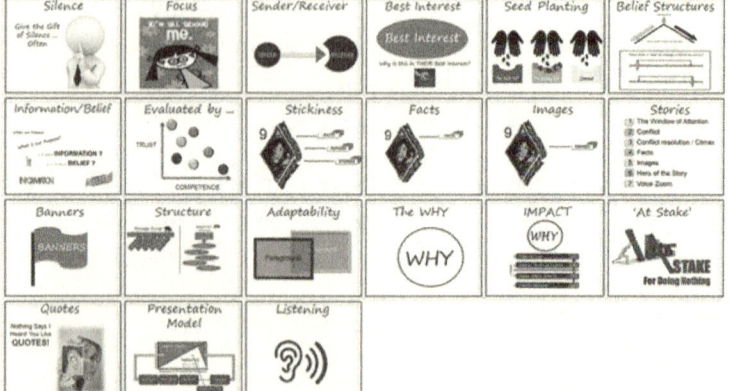

Art of Questions

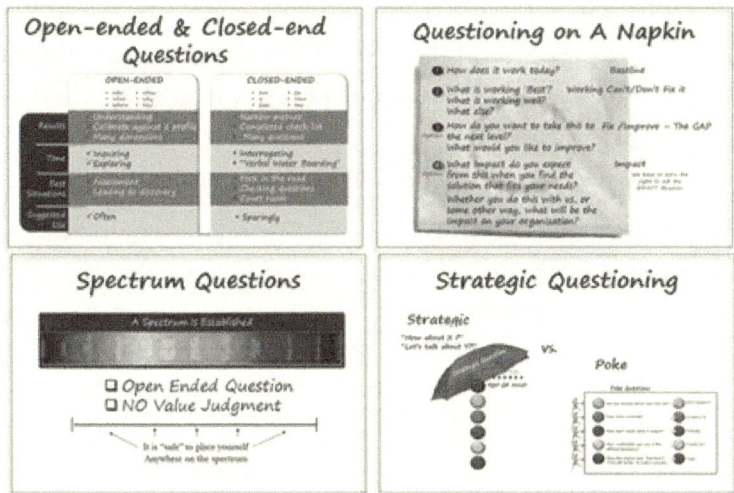

"So if our mission is to improve our communications today, let's start with one of the most powerful ways to improve as a communicator." She advanced the slide.

The Gift of Silence

"What is the gift of silence?" She took two steps closer to the audience while she counted silently to herself.

"We might define the gift of silence as follows: after we make a statement or ask a question, instead of merely rambling on, we remain silent."

She waited while they chewed on the definition. "My guess is that we can all think of situations in the last forty-eight hours where folks have just rambled about something for five minutes or more when they probably should have kept their words to about thirty seconds. Most of us feel very uncomfortable with silence." She waited, then asked, "So what do we do?"

The participants responded, "Fill the silence."

"Correct, we fill the *space* with babble, with garbage, with many words. Even when we ask questions, we tend to fill the space. This is a classic way we ask questions, because we are uncomfortable with silence, **'How is the new job? Do you like it? Is it similar to what you were doing before? What is the name of the company?'**"

Christa silently counted to five. Then she asked, "What is a better way to ask questions about someone's new job?"

The audience threw out a few suggestions. She responded, "Correct, yes, it would be better if we asked, 'How is the new job?' And then gave the gift of silence."

Surveying the audience from left to right, she asked, "Why the gift of silence?"

Participants shouted out some reasons, "We learn more." "It is more respectful." "Few people do it, so it is more inviting."

She smiled. "Well done. On the money. The best communication is a dialogue, not a monologue. The gift of silence creates space to invite dialogue." She waited and counted to five before asking, "After we make a statement or ask a question, how long should we wait before we fill the silence if they don't fill it?"

Again, the participants volunteered their estimates, "Until you can't stand it." "Count to ten." "Count to five." "When they start to squirm." Some of the group showed disapproval of the last response by shaking their heads.

Christa looked across the room with a tightness in her eyes. "None of what we discuss today should be used to manipulate folks or to make folks feel uncomfortable. We certainly don't want folks to squirm. We want to create a safe space for dialogue and make folks feel they have been heard."

She wanted to let her comment about manipulation find its way through the group.

"The gift of silence is very hard. For some of us, waiting three seconds will feel like an eternity, but five seconds is a good goal. The gift of silence radically changes the tone of the discussion and the effectiveness of the communications."

Christa could feel there was some discomfort in the audience as the participants tried to imagine counting to five after a statement or question. She waited for reactions. She pointed to a person who obviously had something to share. She listened to the participant. She thanked him. Then she looked for another who wanted to share their thoughts.

She stood attentively and listened as the participants spoke. "Thank you for sharing your thoughts on the gift of silence.

"Last year, I had the privilege of working with a leadership group every month for eleven months. In our first session, we talked about the gift of silence. One of the men in the group, Seth, who was a self-espoused talker, said, 'Wow, this is so challenging for me. I am not sure I can do this gift of silence thing.'" Christa relieved the moment with a smile. "I suggested to Seth that he consider giving the gift of silence to his wife first."

The audience at Babson instinctively groaned, and some uncomfortably laughed.

"My monthly group had the same reaction you all just did. But Seth said he would give it a try.

"The next month, when we met, Seth raised his hand at the beginning of the meeting. He said, 'I have an update on giving the gift of silence. After we met, I tried giving the gift of silence to my wife at dinner. She asked, **"Seth, are you having an affair?"**'" The audience at Babson laughed. Christa continued with Seth's story. "'I told my wife I had learned the gift of silence in my class. She said, **"Great. Please keep giving me the gift. I like it."** About two weeks later, my wife and I were having a bit of a disagreement about what to do with a kid issue, and she said to me, **"Seth, what happened to the gift of silence?"'** The gift of silence works." She made eye contact up and down the room. "Any questions on the gift of silence before we move on?"

A hand went up on the right, in the back. "Can you give the gift of silence over the phone?"

Christa nodded. "Yes, as we all know, the phone naturally creates more cross-talk because we can't pick up on a person's body language when he or she is finished. Actually, the gift of silence reduces some of this talking over each other." She waited for them to digest the thought. "After we introduced the gift of silence to a client, we occasionally might hear during phone meetings, 'Are you still there' or 'is this the gift of silence?'" There were some chuckles.

The Gift of Silence

"People are unaccustomed to the gift of silence. But the gift of silence is powerful, inviting, and helps us step out of the natural 'me, me, me mode.'"

"Speaking about the 'me, me, me' mode, let's shift to the next topic. Our focus."

A new image is shown on the screen.

"The problem with 'me, me, me.'"

"Today, to be better communicators, perhaps our greatest challenge is to get the stain out of the carpet of 'me, me, me.'"

"I would like to think of myself as empathetic and caring, so I must certainly *not* be one of those communicators who is 'all about me.' But no dice, I am constantly challenged to get myself out of the way, to create a picture for folks where my thumb is not on the lens. To edit my communications so they are *not* all about me."

17

A list appeared on the screen. "Let's look at this list of 'all about me' communication behaviors. Every time I go through this list, I find it incredibly indicting."

- **Air Time:** *we dominate it*
- **Silence:** *we give no gifts of silence*
- **Questions:** *few, if any, questions*
- **Questions:** *closed-ended/controlling*
- **Messaging:** *the pitch—spaghetti on the wall*
- **Messaging:** *standard pitch, not tailored messages*
- **Empathy:** *void or minimal*
- **Pronouns:** *I dominates*
- **Interrupting:** *our controlling weapon of choice*
- **Objectives:** *we can't articulate their objectives*
- **Priorities:** *we can't articulate their priorities*
- **Agenda:** *our agenda is not a collaborative agenda*
- **Perceived Success:** *our view: "veni, vidi, vici" vs. their view: "they came, they listened, they understood"*

"Let's look at each of these briefly."

Air Time: We Dominate It

"What do you think we mean by air time?"

There were several definitions offered by the audience.

"Well done. Net-net, we define air time as the amount of time and attention units we get or take. How often have you sat in a meeting with more than a dozen people and one or two of the folks absolutely and inappropriately dominate the air time? Sometimes, it seems that people merely fall in love with the sound of our own voice."

Silence: We Give No Gifts of Silence

The Gift of Silence

"We already addressed this. I hope you all try the gift of silence."

Questions: *Few, if Any, Questions*
Questions: *Closed-Ended/Controlling*

"Questions are an indicator of whether or not we are in the *ask* mode or the *tell* mode. Closed-ended checking questions can be as effective, but when we use closed-ended questions to control folks, it is as ineffective as being in the *tell* mode. Questions are a critical part of effective communication. We will spend some more time discussing questions this afternoon."

Messaging: *The Pitch—Spaghetti on the Wall*
Messaging: *Standard Pitch, Not Tailored Messages*

"How do we deliver our messages to clients, prospects, or colleagues? Do we just throw a potpourri of messages on the wall like spaghetti and see what sticks? Do we have the same pitch we use over and over again, or do we tailor and customize our messages to the audience?"

Empathy: *Void or Minimal*

"Have we put ourselves in their shoes—the folks with whom we are trying to communicate? What do they want to discuss? How do they want to be engaged in the conversation?"

Pronouns: I Dominates

"I had a very interesting opportunity a couple years ago. I was meeting with a client group monthly. For our third session together, the client brought in an expert on Myers Briggs for the morning. It was fun. I got to listen and watch while the consultant facilitated.

"I had one woman in the group with a serious air time and 'me, me, me' problem. Let's call her Ann. I decided that since I had an unusual opportunity to observe, I would calibrate how bad Ann's problem was. We had fifteen people in the group. Near the beginning of the Myers Briggs session, I started to count how many times Ann felt obligated to share her 'earth-shattering' opinions or 'unique' thoughts with the group and how many times she used the pronoun *I*. I kept a tally for the first hour." Then Christa extended her arms to the audience. "How many times do you think Ann spoke her mind in the first hour, and how many times did she use the pronoun *I*?"

The audience offered their estimates for the number of *I*s, "Six." "Five." "Ten." "Three." "Twelve."

"Thanks for your answers. In one hour, Ann spoke her mind and interrupted the facilitator eight times and used thirty-seven *I*s!"

There was gasp in the front of the room. "Counting her *I*s made me so upset, I had to stop after an hour."

Someone in the audience shouted, "Did you tell her?"

Christa put her head down. "I had a one-on-one conversation with her—as I regularly did with everyone in the group. Ann and I had an uncomfortable conversation. She was embarrassed, unaware, and pretty appalled at her behavior. To Ann's credit, through the rest of the year, she worked really hard on managing her air time and curbing her 'me, me, me.' She also got pretty good at inviting the introverts to step up and take some air time.

"Let's talk about the next thing on the list: interrupting."

Interrupting: Our Controlling Weapon of Choice

"This is a very common weapon of control in communication. We use it at home. We use it with direct reports, we use it with colleagues. To our own peril, we sometimes use it with customers and the folks above us.

"We need to eliminate interrupting from our arsenal. We need to expunge its variants like 'cropping.'" She paused for a moment to let the image rest with the audience. "Cropping is where we finish other people's sentences for them."

She gave the gift of silence to the audience.

"I find this tough stuff, uncomfortable reminders that it too often is 'all about me.'"

She walked to the back of the stage area and pointed to the screen.

"Let's take these next three together."

Objectives: We Can't Articulate Their Objectives
Priorities: We Can't Articulate Their Priorities
Agenda: Our Agenda Is Not a Collaborative Agenda

"I hear from executives, client teams, and sales teams all the time things, like 'We are really "in touch" with our people or with our clients or customers.'

"Yet when we ask teams to articulate the objectives and priorities of their clients, there tends to be a loud thud. When we ask teams to provide meeting agendas they have used with clients, the agendas are typically all about them and not client-focused."

Perceived Success: *Our View: "Veni, Vidi, Vici" vs. Their View: "They Came, They Listened, They Understood"*

"The last way to calibrate our 'all about me' tendencies is to ask ourselves, What do we perceive as success in meetings with clients, prospects, or colleagues? Is success 'veni, vidi, vici'—we came, we saw, we conquered–or is it we came, we listened, we understood?

"Checking our tendencies at making communications 'all about me' is very hard, but it is imperative if we want to be more effective communicators.

"This note works great tacked on our PC or the wall in our office. It is a great litmus test for our communications."

"Every time we draft an email or prepare for a call or a meeting, we should look at our words and our messages and ask, Who is this about? Is this communication about me or is it about them?"

Chapter 3

After a very short break, Christa walked to the front of the room with three whiteboard markers in her hands.

"So we talked about two communication topics so far:

> One, evaluating and calibrating our communications to see if our communications are 'all about me.'

> Two, we talked about giving the gift of silence as a tool for good communication.

"Any questions?

"Great!"

Then without warning, Christa threw one of the markers at an athletic-looking man in a black sweater in his thirties in the sixth row on the right. The marker flew past him as he tried to catch it.

There were some uncomfortable chuckles in the room as almost everyone was confused as to why Christa threw the marker at this young man.

Christa, without saying a word, locked eye contact with the young man and held up her right hand with another marker. The man in the black sweater put his open hands in front of his chest and braced for another throw of the marker.

Christa threw the second marker, and the young man caught it.

Christa said, "Nice catch."

Turning to the audience as a whole, she said, "Tell me what just went on here?"

The audience answered, "You threw something for some reason." "You threw the marker." "You caught him off guard." "You almost killed him."

Christa turned to the young man, "What happened?"

He said, "I missed the first marker you threw at me, and I caught the second marker you threw at me."

Christa smiled again. "Yes, you almost caught the first one too. Thanks for letting me do that. It is Jon, right?" she said, looking at the name on his tent card.

"Jon, why do you think I threw the markers at you?"

The young man squirmed a bit, then said, "I don't know. Maybe it looked like I wasn't paying attention, but I was."

Christa shook her head. "No. I know you were paying attention. If I threw the marker at you because you weren't paying attention, I might have thrown it a lot harder."

The group laughed.

Christa began again, "Let's, for a moment, say that the markers represent a message we want to send. The first marker I threw is the typical and the classic way we send messages. We just launch them, we throw them at folks without preparing them to catch them or to receive them."

Still addressing the young man, "Tell me the difference between the first and the second marker I threw."

The young man laughed. "The first one, I muffed. The second one, I caught."

"Jon, tell me about your heart rate. If we had a heart monitor on you when these markers were thrown to you, what would it have told us about your heart rate?"

Jon pointed up. "My heart rate probably spiked."

"Right. When would your heart rate have spiked more, on the first throw or the second throw?"

He held up one finger. "The first throw. On the second throw, you let me know with your eyes and your hand that you were throwing the second marker. I was ready for it. I was pretty relaxed—except that you are a girl with not that great an arm, and I didn't know where the heck the throw was going."

The audience groaned.

Christa was caught off guard. "Okay, so much for politically correct comments in our workshop. By the way, my dad would be pretty dismayed to hear that comment because he spent many an hour throwing the ball around with me."

She let the lightheartedness fade.

"Back to our metaphor."

She held up the third marker, which she still had in her hand. "So the reason for doing this marker thing is to demonstrate the most basic and impactful principle of communication, the *sender/receiver principle.* There is the sender of the message, and there is the receiver of the message. Unfortunately, the most typical way we send a message is we just throw the message at the receiver whether they are prepared or ready to receive it . . . or not!

Still holding up the marker, she continued, "The first time I threw the marker to Jon, he had no warning nor preparation. Based upon having done these hundreds of times, his chances of catching the first marker were less than 30 percent. The second time I threw it, he was ready. He gave me tacit permission with his eyes. He readied his hands to catch it. The chances of him catching the second marker were 80 percent or better.

"Make sense?" She opened her hands expressing vulnerability and openness.

She took a moment and consciously gave the gift of silence.

"Another way of looking at this principle is playing catch. We have the thrower—the sender of the message. We have the ball—the message—and we have the catcher—the receiver of the message. If we are playing catch with someone, we want to make sure that they are ready and able to catch the ball. If we merely throw the ball at them without them being ready, (a) they are unlikely to catch it, or (b) we might even hurt them."

She stopped and surveyed the room. "Consider the norm when we send an important message. How often do we calibrate whether or not the receiver is ready to receive the message?" She paused. "How often do we prepare the receiver to catch the message to improve the odds it will stick? So perhaps you are thinking, 'I get it. We need to do a better job ensuring that folks we catch our message, but how?'

"Let's talk about two simple ways to improve the odds that someone is ready to receive our message: First, calibrate. Second, use some specific readiness approaches. How do we calibrate?" She let the question marinate for a moment. "Before we send an important message, we embrace the discipline of asking ourselves, How ready is this person or these people to receive this message?

"What if the little voice in our head says, they are *not* ready?"

The audience shouted a wide range of responses.

"You can see, we have varying thoughts about this. What is the right approach? That is an art question. You each need to practice your own art and captain your own ship in these situations. Whether we choose to hold our message until they are ready or proceed anyway, the sender/receiver principle is in play: when it is clear someone is not ready to receive our message, the odds that they will embrace, receive, or catch the message is very low.

"This begs the next question you are likely to have: How can we improve the odds that we can get them ready? Here are four readiness approaches that can help. Develop your own phrasing and your own talk track."

The screen showed the following:

One of the questions I thought you might have is . . .

How helpful would it be if I explained . . .

May I/we put something on the table for consideration. . .

May I have your permission to . . .

"Here are four specific approaches to ready the receiver of the message. The first is, 'One of the questions I thought you might have is . . .' This lets the receiver know that you have tried to be empathetic and look at things from their perspective.

"The second is, 'How helpful would it be if I explained . . .' This works exceptionally well when you are about to answer an objection or clarify something is murky. It improves the odds that someone really does want an explanation. It is imperative that when we ask, 'How helpful would it be if I explained XYZ?' that we follow it with the gift of silence. This pause allows us to further calibrate their readiness by their verbal or nonverbal response.

"The third approach is, 'May I/we put something on the table for consideration. . .' This approach works well when we are about to coach someone or make a suggestion in a sensitive area. One of the reasons it works is because it subtly implies that you are putting something on the buffet for them to select or not—to ingest or not.

"Finally, another approach is 'May I have your permission to . . .' This works in situations where we are likely to be treading into dangerous waters—addressing a delicate area.

"This is the sender/receiver principle. It is simple and fundamental yet powerful in helping us become better communicators. We need to understand it, and we can improve our application of it by employing the discipline of calibrating—asking how ready they are to receive the message, and by using the readiness approaches we discussed."

Best Interest

"Let's move on to the next topic, the best interest principle." Christa deepened her breathing to extricate herself from past nightmares of the story she had brought to the table. She worked to be fully present with her audience.

"One of the most common questions I get in coaching sessions is, '**What are the best ways to get so-and-so onboard about what we are trying to do?**' What might a good answer be?"

The audience chimed in with "Show them the logic." "Demonstrate ROI." "Have someone else convince them." "Make it politically smart." "Make them think it is their idea." "Get their boss onboard." "Make them think they are a leader." "Make them think they are getting on the bandwagon." "Bribe them." "Break their kneecaps." "Tell their mother."

Seeing the downhill pattern of the last comments, Christa gestured to stop. "Okay, when I am asked that question, my answer is almost always '**Tell me why it is in their** *best interest* **to get onboard.**' If we can't identify why it is in someone's best interest to get onboard, what right do we have to expect their support?

"This is the best interest principle. It is so simple yet so missing. It is absent in the workplace, it is rare with clients, it is even often missing at home.

"Very few people demonstrate empathy or take the time to understand why it is *your* best interest"—pointing to the left side of the room—"or *your* best interest"—pointed to the middle of the room—"or *your* best interest"—pointing to the right side of the room—"to join the parade.

"If I can encourage us to pick one question to make the norm in our organization—a question to make a cornerstone of our culture, it is 'Help me understand why or how it is in their best interest?' This question drives so many good communication habits of a client-centered culture."

She paused. "Any questions on best interest?" After waiting for questions and receiving none, she moved to the next topic.

Seed Planting

"Let's talk next about seed planting. Think about how often we are trying to get our internal team members, our bosses, our clients, and our prospects to *buy into* what we are saying. We are trying to plant some messages, which we hope will take root. We are trying to plant messages, which will be embraced and even grow."

Christa advanced the slide.

Planting Messages

The Rich Soil
It is about 'Them'
- Their Stated Objectives
- Their Words
- Their Key Initiatives
- Their Specific Needs

The Rocky Soil
It is about 'People Like Them'
- We take educated guesses about their needs
- We explain functional ways we meet the 'needs' we think they might have
- We provide general 'Industry trends' information
- We talk about 'People Who Might Be Like Them'

Cement
It is about 'Us'
- This is why we are great
- This is how we work
- This is how 'smart' we are
- This is why we own the market
- This is why you would be foolish not to buy from us or foolish not to listen to us

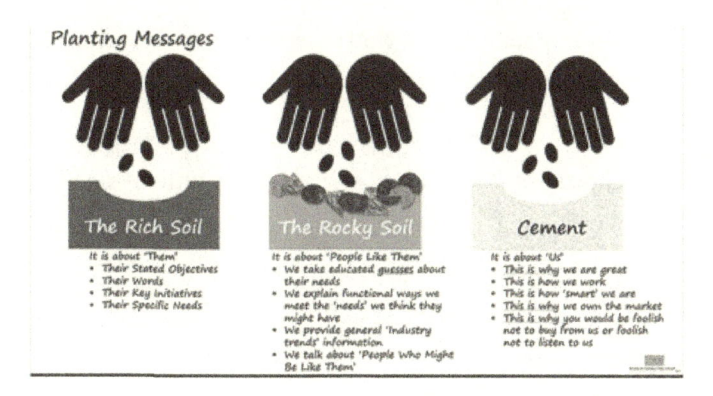

"We see three different approaches to seed planting, whether it is planting messages externally or internally.

"The first approach to planting seeds is the cement approach. We simply drop our messages onto the cement."

Showing the slide, Christa continued, "This approach is characterized by *'it is about us.'* There is typically an arrogance or hubris in the delivery of messages with an undertone of

> this is why we are great,
> this is how we work,
> this is how 'smart' we are,
> this is why we own the market—if talking to prospects—and
> this is why you would be foolish not to buy from us or foolish not to listen to us.

"For most folks, this is not the default approach for delivering messages. Still, every one of us has been on the receiving end of messages delivered with a clear screeching tone of the 'I am the smartest person in the room' or 'you'd be foolish not to listen to me.'"

She paused for a moment. "How do those messages feel when we receive them? How much do those messages inspire us to embrace them?"

There was a chorus of "not good, unattractive, uninviting, frustrating, resist them."

"Exactly. Let's move on to the rocky soil approach to messaging. This is, by far, the most common approach to messaging today.

"Rocky soil messaging can land some messages, but rocky soil messages can also miss. We call it the rocky soil approach because some of the messages, indeed, fall into the rich soil and grow, and some of the messages fall on the rocks and die a quick death.

"Rocky soil messaging is characterized by *'people like them.'* Typically, *we take educated guesses about the audience's needs.* We get some of the guesses right. We miss with some of our messages.

"When presenting our messages to prospects, the rocky soil approach gravitates to things like *industry trends* and the pundits, say XYZ. As an example, let's look at a sales team selling in healthcare. A study might show that healthcare organizations today are rapidly moving to a different value-based reimbursement model.

"The sales team is given this study. They show up at a new prospect healthcare system, having done little or no discovery about the specific approach of that healthcare system to reimbursement. The sales team jumps into the rocky soil mode. The team quotes the study. They plant many messages about how they can help with value-based care. Meanwhile, the healthcare participants are sitting there thinking, *Don't they know us?* True, the pundits say value-based care is the trend, but it is *not* our trend. These people don't know us at all.

"Another problem with rocky soil messaging is that, many times, it is highly focused on *how* we do things rather than *why* it is in their best interest to take action. We explain functional ways we meet the needs we think they might have. Going back to the previous example, the sales team might compound their messaging error by spending valuable minutes of their meeting time on the seventeen ways they can help implement value-based care.

"Again, this is the most common approach to planting messages, and it has its merits. But it misses quite often, it doesn't feel personal, and it doesn't work nearly as well as the rich soil messaging.

"So what is rich soil messaging? Rich soil messaging *is about them*. We talk about *their stated objectives*. We use *their words*. We focus on *their key initiatives*. We address *their specific needs*.

"Rich soil messages work because they are grounded in the things the audience has explicitly and implicitly told us that are important to them. We are meeting them where they are at. We are not trying to draw their attention or energies to something else. We are providing fuel for the things that are already on their radar, things that they stated were important to them.

"Clearly, rich soil messaging requires deeper empathy and deeper discovery. Because of the limits of time, access, and expertise, we can't always plant our messages in the rich soil, but when we do, we are immensely more effective in planting our messages.

"When we examine the messages we are trying to plant with colleagues, clients, or prospects, what kind are they? Are we taking the road most traveled or the road with many detours? Are we planting in the rocky soil? Or are we planting our messages into their words, their needs, their priorities, and their stated objectives?

"The rich soil takes discipline, but it is orders of magnitude more effective in terms of messaging."

Chapter 4

Belief Structures

Christa transitioned to the next topic. "Belief structures. Why discuss belief structures?

"Just a few years ago, I used to get questions from workshop participants struggling to understand why belief structures are so important to effective communications. Bless the politics of today for teaching us this lesson. Few in our country today would argue that wherever you are on the political spectrum, there is little trust and respect for those who hold a different position. Each position demonizes the other position. There is little, if any, change or compromise in any of the political positions or views.

"Why is this an important recognition for us? Here is a metaphorical picture of a belief structure."

"These belief structures, depending on how strong they are, are either made of brick, wood, or straw—to borrow from the three little pigs.

"We often have misconceptions about how the brain works: A person has a belief, and we think we can change their belief merely by giving them the right information. This is a common and, particularly, a pernicious paradigm in high-tech, 'If I just give you the right data, the right benchmarks, the right ROI model, the right case studies, then you will get it.'

"Unfortunately, that is not how the brain works.

"More accurately, this information is like a raindrop falling on the peak of the roof of our belief structure. Depending upon our beliefs, we push the information to one side or the other to support and affirm our existing belief structure.

"So as an example, if you are politically far right, and you are presented with information and ideas from the far left, you will dismiss the information as fake news at best.

"Similarly, if you are politically far left, and you are presented with information and ideas from the far right, you will dismiss the information as contrived at best."

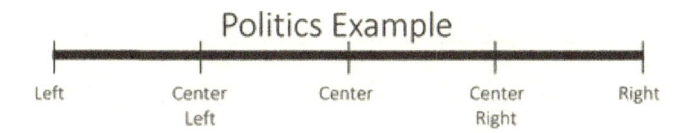

Politics Example

Left | Center Left | Center | Center Right | Right

"Take a moment and think about one person you know by name who was on the far left and moved to the far right, or one person you know by name who was on the far right and moved to the far left.

"Having asked the question of thousands of people, I have six names, and two of them are Canadians."

The audience laughed.

"Part of our responsibility in communicating effectively is to calibrate where people are in terms of their belief structures and how far we might be able to move them."

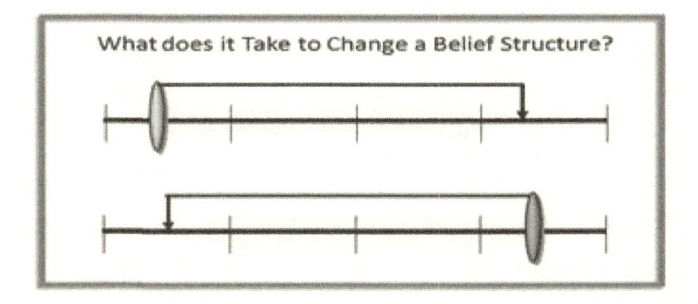

What does it Take to Change a Belief Structure?

"Just like in the politics question, we are very unlikely to move people from one end of the spectrum to the other end of the spectrum. Unfortunately, in business, we try to accomplish a radical change in belief all the time."

What does it Take to Change a Belief Structure?

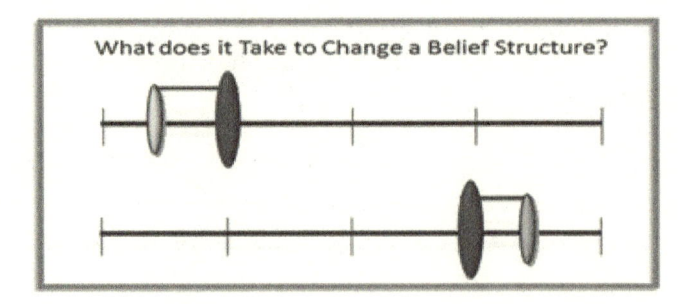

"Even though we need to eschew the trap of trying to transform beliefs from one end of the spectrum to another, indeed, it is our responsibility to move people and to impact belief structures in realistic ways.

"So when we think about belief structures, we need to *calibrate* the belief structures of those with whom we are communicating. We need to determine how much we can realistically impact their beliefs. We need to chart a course to effectively move them based upon our calibration."

Christa opened her left hand to the audience. "What questions do you have about this?"

The audience posed several specific situational questions, which Christa addressed.

"Before we move on, let's talk about one more important element of belief structures: our own belief structures and how they are contagious. Our own belief structures impact the receiver in embracing our message.

"When I was young and had been in my first management/leadership role for a little over a month, one of my direct reports, Tom Hudson, came into my office and closed the door behind him. Tom was twenty-five years older than I was at the time. He was a wonderful man and very wise. He said to me, 'Christa, you know that everyone on the team takes their temperature from yours. When you are hot about things, they are hot. When you are cold on ideas and approaches, they are cold.'

"This really stuck with me. I see it in communications all the time, where the sender's message tips their hand about a belief structure that is not aligned with the message they are trying to send. The receiver of the message picks up on the unspoken belief structures. The receiver takes their temperature from the sender's beliefs and not the sender's messages."

Advancing the slide, she continued, "Here are just some of the situations where we have all seen folks take their temperature from the beliefs of the communicator and not their words."

Christa gave the group time to read each quote. "Which of these resonate most with you?"

There was a brief dialogue about the list.

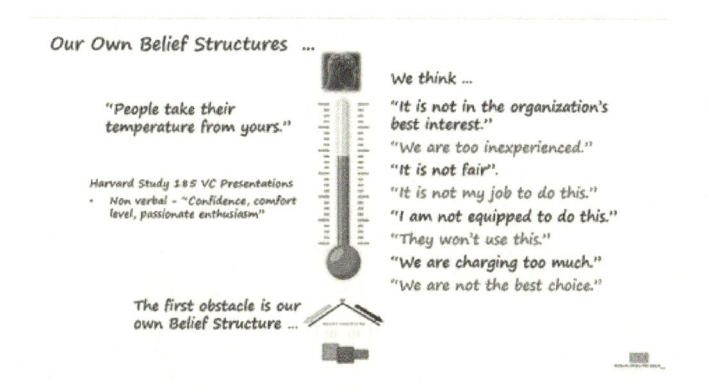

Our Own Belief Structures ...

"People take their temperature from yours."

Harvard Study 185 VC Presentations
- Non verbal – "Confidence, comfort level, passionate enthusiasm"

The first obstacle is our own Belief Structure ...

We think ...
"It is not in the organization's best interest."
"We are too inexperienced."
"It is not fair".
"It is not my job to do this."
"I am not equipped to do this."
"They won't use this."
"We are charging too much."
"We are not the best choice."

"Along these lines, there was a study done looking at 185 Venture Capital Presentations, and which presentations captured investments and which ones did not. The most important attributes in gaining financial support from investors after these presentations were not the dollars and cents, opportunity, nor the experience of the presenters. It was the nonverbal confidence, comfort level, and passionate enthusiasm of the presenters, which was the most common thread in gaining funding. The investors took their temperature from that of the presenters.

"Call it what you like—alignment, integrity, the metaphysical ether—we need to make sure we have checked and scrutinized our own belief structures before we carry a message.

"We need to recognize that, indeed, folks take their temperature from ours."

Chapter 5

Information or Belief?

"One of the most common objectives for people attending this workshop is to be more effective in presenting the material. So based upon what we have discussed so far, when we present to either colleagues internally or clients externally, what is the purpose of our presentation?

"Is it about information or about belief?"

Christa showed her slide.

When we Present ...
What is our Purpose?
Is it about **INFORMATION ?**
Or is it about **BELIEF ?**

NO MATION   BELIEF

The audience offered a few different answers: "It depends on the situation."

"It is about the right information." "It is both." "Sometimes, it is about belief."

Christa smiled. She recognized that the group was progressing well in their thinking about communication. "If we want to be as effective as we can in presenting, we need to remember—" She hesitated and waved her arms broadly as to wipe away the smoke of confusion. "It is always about belief!" She raised her voice to almost a shout.

Then she gave the gift of silence.

She continued in her normal voice, "We need to think about which beliefs we want our audience to embrace. Then we can choose the information that is most likely to support those beliefs."

She let the statement sit for a moment.

Christa put her head down and took four steps to the right. She lifted up her head, then said, "We have spent a couple hours together. None of what we have discussed, none of the approaches we looked at to improve communications, or approaches we *will* look at to improve communications will make any sense. None of them will stick if we don't *believe* that, number one, we need to get 'all about me' out of our communications, and number two, we need to change our focus to *them*. We need to understand specifically how our suggestions or recommendations are in *their best interest*. These beliefs and these paradigms drive our approaches. These beliefs are the glue that holds every recommended change we are discussing. The way we think about something impacts how others react to what we say."

She surveyed the audience to calibrate how well this point had landed.

One participant, Mari, raised her hand and said, "Sorry, Christa, I don't get this. We have a weekly meeting where we each go through the state of the business. This meeting is all about information."

Christa smiled warmly at the participant making the point. "Good point, Mari. May I have your permission to take a brief bird walk?" Christa was conscious that she was demonstrating the sender/receiver principle.

Mari nodded. Christa continued, "A number of years ago, when I had one of my first management positions, I had a boss, Lou, who was a genius with spreadsheets. He had twelve managers reporting to him, and he decided to hold these monthly in-person meetings, where each manager would stand up and report on the state of our business with a spreadsheet. We went in alphabetical order to present, so one of the guys on the team, whose name was Mark, went first. Mark was extremely affable, everyone loved him personally, but he was not a good detail guy and perhaps not the smartest tack in the drawer. Mark would get up first with his spreadsheet and present the state of his business. As Mark presented, Lou would do some of the spreadsheet calculations in his head. Within five minutes, Lou would find a fatal flaw in Mark's calculations. Then Lou's hair would catch fire, he would jump into his Spanish inquisition mode, and for the rest of the day, Lou would verbally beat the tar out of each of us as we went through our presentations."

Christa walked across the front of the room, opened her arms, and asked the group, "What do you think was happening?"

The participants offered a few suggestions, and then someone shouted, "Lou didn't believe Mark!"

Christa pointed enthusiastically at the person making the suggestion and exclaimed, "Bingo! Right on the money. Lou didn't believe that Mark knew his business, and since he didn't believe Mark knew his business, he extrapolated that none of us knew our business.

"Mark never understood that this monthly exercise was a test of belief—how much did Lou *believe* that each of us knew our business? Mark thought it was about presenting the information. So he inadvertently started us down a slippery slope right into Lou's pit of despair and a belief by Lou that his team was clueless and incompetent."

She turned to the audience again. "So how do you think we fixed this?"

Again, the audience provided suggestions. "You taught Mark how to set up formulas in Excel." "You checked Mark's work before he presented." "You got Mark fired." The group groaned at the last suggestion.

Christa shook her head. "We did try to help Mark with his spreadsheet skills, but we changed the tone of these meetings 180 degrees by simply asking Lou to go in reverse alphabetical order so that Mark went last."

Christa summarized, "Net-net, we need to keep reminding ourselves that when we present, it is always about belief!"

Christa turned to Mari, who had posed the question, and said, "Did I answer your question?"

Mari said, "Yes, thank you."

How We Are Evaluated

"Let's spend a few moments talking about what we mean by 'selling.' In the strictest form, *Webster's Third* defines it as

selling *n-s* (ME, fr. gerund of *sellen* to sell)

1: the act of one who sells. 2: the act, process, or art of offering goods for sale

"Most of us here spend a considerable amount of time and effort trying to get colleagues, bosses, clients, and even family members to support our ideas or plans. We are trying to get 'buy-in.' So in essence, we are selling them on the idea or plan.

"*Webster* defines the colloquial use of 'buy-in' as . . .

buy-in

1: acceptance of and willingness to actively support and participate in something (such as a proposed new plan or policy)

"We will take a look at one view of how folks evaluate us when we are selling them an idea or selling them a product or a solution. Let's do a fun little exercise."

Would You Buy From ... ?

"I would like the left side of the room to take row *A*, so numbers 1 to 10. The middle of the room to take row *B*—numbers 11 to 20. The right side of the room to take row *C*—numbers 21 to 30.

"Here is what I would like each of you to do: Very quickly, write down whether or not you would buy from each of the people in your assigned row. So if you have row *A*, write down if you would buy from number one or two, etc. You can only answer yes or no. There can be no maybes. I know some of you want to ask me, What are they selling? But we can't answer that. This is a blink exercise, so do it very quickly—don't overthink it."

Christa walked around the room observing different reactions. She waited for everyone to finish their quick evaluations.

"Okay, raise your hand if you would buy from number one." She demonstrated by raising her own hand. "Number two? Number three?" There were a wide variety of responses to the first three faces in the exercise. "By the way, there are no right and wrong answers here. There are just patterns, which we will discuss at the end of the exercise."

Christa continued down the row asking for their responses. When she got to number six, the woman with the dark hair in the circle, she stopped and smiled. "By the way, she is, by far and away, the face that gets the most 'Yes, I would buy' from her responses." Christa quickly continued the querying process down the row. She stopped again at number ten. "I see that not many people would buy from Don Draper," referring to the iconic *Mad Men* image.

She rifled through row *B*, stopping for a moment at number twenty, the young man with a beard, glasses, and spiked hair. She said, "I did this exercise last year, and I had this guy, Howie, who had row *B* like you. Howie looked just like the picture. Interestingly, he said he won't buy from him." The room laughed.

She quickly went through row *C*. When she got to number twenty-six, the attractive young woman with the red lipstick, only one young man in the eighth row on the right put his hand up. There were a few under-the-breath chuckles. Christa looked at him and smiled acceptingly. "Your honesty is duly noted."

"So you can see that the answers you gave are all over the board. There are no right or wrong answers, they are *your* answers. The people from whom *you* would or would not buy."

She waited a moment to get affirmation from the audience.

"So what are the patterns?

"In answering the blink question of 'Would you buy from this person?' we each have two things we weigh in varying degrees. We each have our own individual balance of how important these two things are to us."

She advanced the slide.

"Those things are trust and competence."

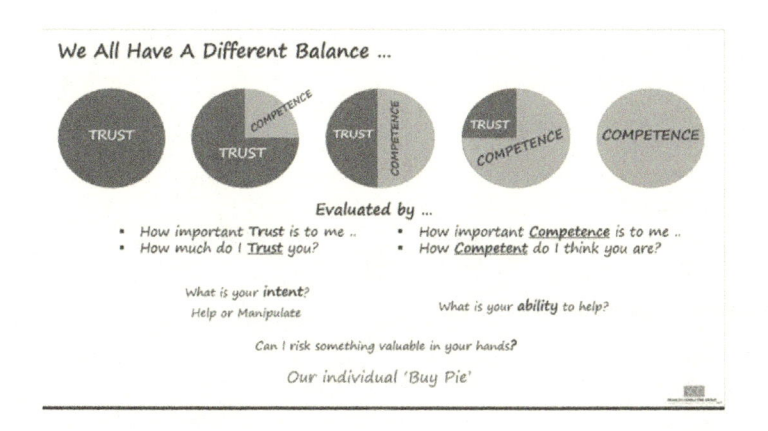

We All Have A Different Balance ...

Evaluated by ...
- How important Trust is to me ..
- How much do I Trust you?
- How important Competence is to me ..
- How Competent do I think you are?

What is your **intent**?
Help or Manipulate

What is your **ability** to help?

Can I risk something valuable in your hands?

Our individual 'Buy Pie'

How important is trust to me?

How much do I trust you?

How important is competence to me?

How competent are you?

She gave the audience a moment to absorb the slide.

"For some folks, it is all about trust. They want to know your intent. Are you going to help me or hurt me? Are you going to help me or manipulate me?

"For others, it is about competence. Their attitude is, 'I can take care of myself.' 'I don't need to worry too much about your intent.' 'I just need to know if you can get the job done.' 'Do you have the ability to help?'

"We each have our own balance of these two elements, which deliver our answer to the question, Would we buy from the person? One client called this individual balance our buy pie.

"Different faces here engender different feelings about trust and competence."

"The folks on the left tend to be viewed as having positive intent. In that way, they tend to be viewed as trustworthy. The faces on the right tend to be viewed as getting the job done but not very high on trust.

"The man with the clenched fist is often viewed as forceful, confident, and competent, but many people question his intent.

"As I mentioned earlier, the young woman in the circle, who is high and to the right, gets the most consistent support in the exercise because she is seen as both trustworthy and competent.

"So given that every one of us has a different balance of what is important in terms of trust or competence—given that each of us has different buy pie, if we want folks to buy into what we are saying or to actually have them buy something from us, where is the *only* right place to be?"

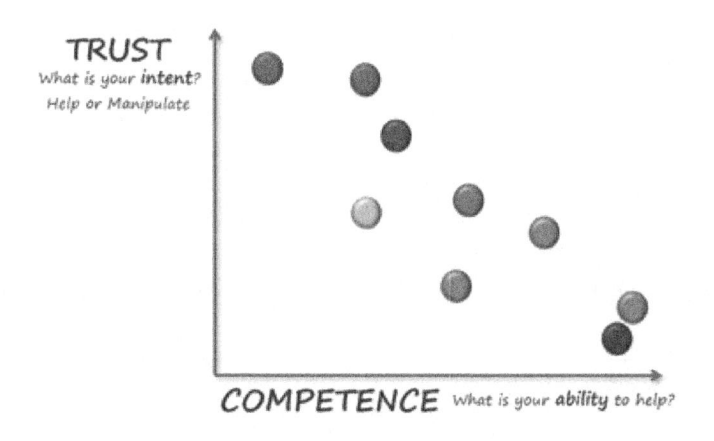

TRUST
what is your **intent**?
Help or Manipulate

COMPETENCE What is your **ability** to help?

She showed the next slide.

Only 'Right Position'

TRUST
What is your intent?
Help or Manipulate

Evaluated by ...
- How much do we **Trust** you?
- How **Competent** are you?

We Need to be Here

COMPETENCE What is your ability to help?

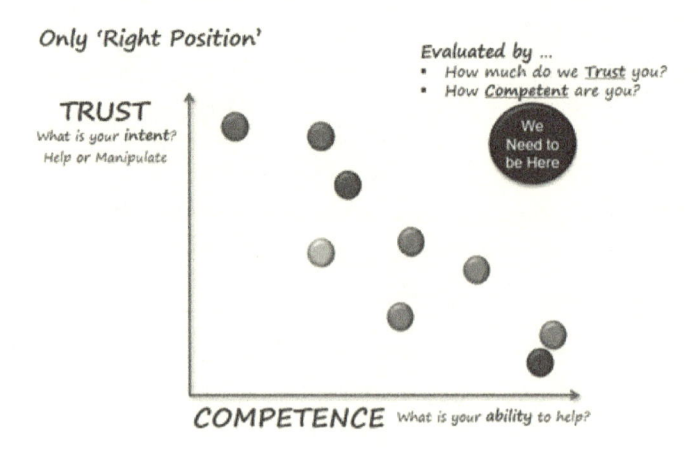

"Correct! The only right place to be is in the top right—to be seen as high in trust and competence. Almost every communication topic we discussed today will help us either with the trust part of this equation and/or the competence part of this equation."

Christa waited for comments. There were a few affirmations and restatements by participants of the points discussed. Then Christa said, "Let's take a break, I will see you in twenty minutes."

At the start of the break, a man who looked very much like her dad approached her. "Christa, so far, I like where you are going with this stuff. It applies not only to challenges we have in business, but I probably would have been a better parent if I had done some of the things we discussed."

She nodded. "Yes. I feel the same way as a parent. It is the most important area and most challenging arena to apply some of these things. I hope that my kids feel as good about my communication with them as I do about my dad's communication with me. I have been very blessed. I learned many of these things from my dad. By the way, as a parent, I think you will particularly the section on questions this afternoon."

"I look forward to it." He walked away.

Christa reached into her pocket, turned on her phone, and sent her dad a text, "Dad, there is a man in my workshop that looks a lot like you. Do we have relatives in Boston? Love you much. Christa."

Chapter 6

Stickiness

"Thank you for your prompt return from the break. The next four sections are highly related. Folks have told me that these sections are some of the most impactful approaches we will discuss today. We are going to discuss stickiness and how the brain works and then some ways to leverage how the brain works by using facts, images, and stories."

Christa advanced the slides. "This is not an anatomy class, I am not an expert on the brain, but it is useful to look at the brain from a layperson's point of view so we can improve the stickiness of our messages."

Pointing to the slide on the screen, she said, "What part of our brain is responsible for most of our memory?"

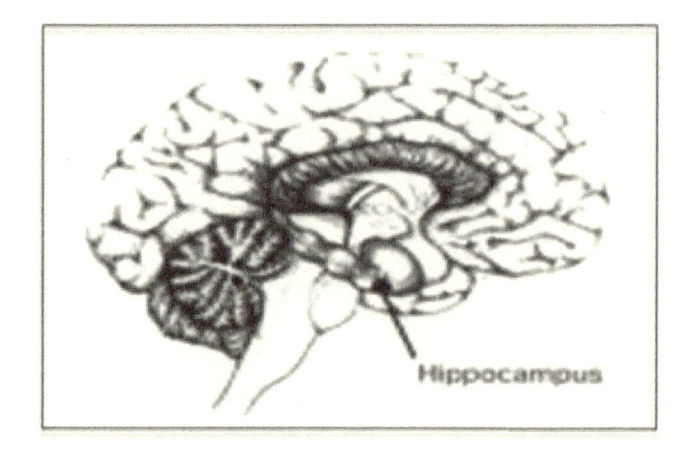

Someone from the audience shouted, "I can't remember." There was laughter. Then someone else observed the answer on the screen. "The hippocampus."

Christa gave a thumbs-up. "Correct. Do we want to remember everything?"

The audience answered uniformly, "No."

She continued, "You are probably aware that there is a disease where a person can see pages of numbers and can remember all of them. Perhaps you remember an old movie with Dustin Hoffman called the *Rain Man*." She waited for some affirmation. "He had a disease, which was previously described as an idiot savant and now is merely described as a savant." She paused. "Why is this a disease? What can't folks do who have this disease?" There was silence. "They can't filter the information. To them, all of the information is the same. A healthy brain filters out information, it doesn't retain everything. So while we are trying to communicate a message to our audience, they are filtering out information. Our brains are processing what to keep and what not to keep . . . what is important? Because it behooves us to understand what is sticky and what is not sticky."

"From a layperson's point of view, the brain has two guards at the gate of the hippocampus. These guards act as filters for what we will keep in memory and what we will retain. Let's look at characteristics of stickiness to better understand what will stick and what will get filtered out. The two guards are association/connection and emotion.

"Let's examine association/connection first. Let's say you are in a place like an airport and you see a face you recognize, but you can't remember the person's name. He/she is not a celebrity. They are someone you know from *your* past. What do you do?"

Again, the participants offered suggestions: "Think of where we know them from." "Tell them they look familiar." "Ask my wife who they are." "I just hide." There was laughter and sidebar comments.

Enjoying the moment with the audience, Christa waited for the group's attention. "Indeed. In this situation, we also try to take inventory. From where do we know this person? From places where we have worked together, from the community, from school, from where we worship, from things we do with our kids, did I date them at some point?"

There were a couple of uncomfortable empathetic chuckles. She continued, "We are looking for the association/connection.

"Association/connection is also how we learn a language. We connect or associate new things with things we already know.

"As mentioned, the other guard at the hippocampus is emotion. We tend to remember things that have an emotional impact. Think through some of the most memorable days of your life. The birth of a child, your wedding, being told you got the job you wanted, the funeral of someone you loved. You can probably picture many detailed things about those moments. You might even remember some of the smells from the experience. Emotions create a powerful imprint on our memory.

"There was a study done at UC Irvine several years ago about the power of emotions on our memories. They tested many people for their ability to recall facts until they built a test group of over a hundred people that was very homogeneous and could recall facts within 1 percent of each other. They then split the group in half and gave each group a story about a fourteen-year-old boy, which was almost identical."

Pointing to the left side of the room, Christa said, "In your version of the story, the fourteen-year-old boy went through travail, but he survived." Then she pointed to the right side of the room. "In your version of the story, everything was identical, the fourteen-year-old boy went through the same travail, but at the end, he died. They tested each for their recall of the facts in the story. The group that had the version where the boy died remembered the facts of the story 50 percent better than the other group, even though they had equal recall ability."

She waited and counted to five in her mind. "Emotions greatly impact the stickiness of our messages.

"So now, let's look at three ways we can leverage our understanding of the brain and its filters of association/connection and emotions. We will look at three ways to *improve the odds* that we will pass through these two filters and create sticky messages."

She took a visible deep breath. "Before we talk about these three things, I want to apologize that I am about to ruin for you the normal listening pleasure of every political speech, talk from the pulpit, college lecture, TED Talk, etc.

"Here are three things we will find in almost all of these talks.

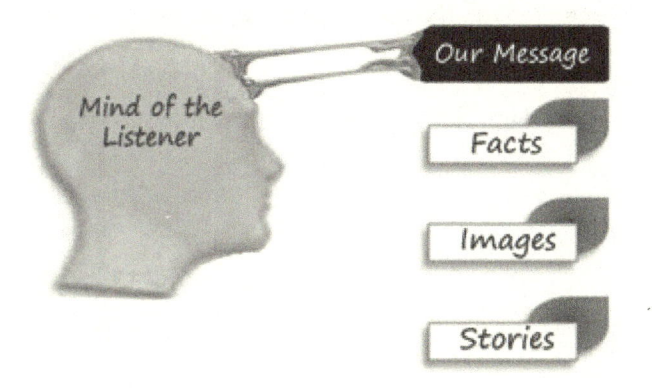

Mind of the Listener

Our Message

Facts

Images

Stories

"Facts, images, and stories.

"We affectionately call these three attributes nine weeping widows. Why nine weeping widows? Because nine is a specific fact, weeping is an image, and every widow has a story.

"Let's look at these one by one. First, facts.

"Most folks do a good job of using specific facts. If you or your organization is left-brain, facts will come quite naturally. We won't spend a great of time here, but let's look at a simple example."

She advanced the slide. "On the left, you have a typical factual statement. **'Many accidents occur after an argument.'** On the right, we use more specific facts, which add to the stickiness. **'One study shows that 59 percent of serious car accidents occur after there has been an argument.'**

TYPICAL STATEMENTS	SAME MESSAGE with FACTS
Many accidents occur after an argument.	One study shows that 59% of serious car accidents occur after there has been an argument.

"These are small changes that improve stickiness. By the way, let's talk about sticky numbers. Which is stickier, 60 percent or 59 percent?"

Everyone in the room affirmed that 59 percent was stickier.

"Which is stickier, the number twenty-five or the number twenty-four?"

The audience was divided about which number was stickier.

"The number twenty-four is more likely to be a sticky number. So what types of numbers should we avoid?"

An older man in the back called out, "Numbers that feel rounded. Ones that end in zero or five."

Christa smiled. "Bingo! Perfect!" She transitioned to the next slide. "Improving stickiness through specific facts and sticky numbers is relatively easy. Images are much harder, but very powerful."

She opened her hand to the audience, inviting an answer to her ensuing question, "Which of these is stickier? She has a real commitment to the work, or she has a real heart for the work?"

Almost everyone affirmed that "heart for the work" was stickier.

She advanced the slide. "There are image words, and there are concept words. Which are stickier?" She paused while some thought and some answered.

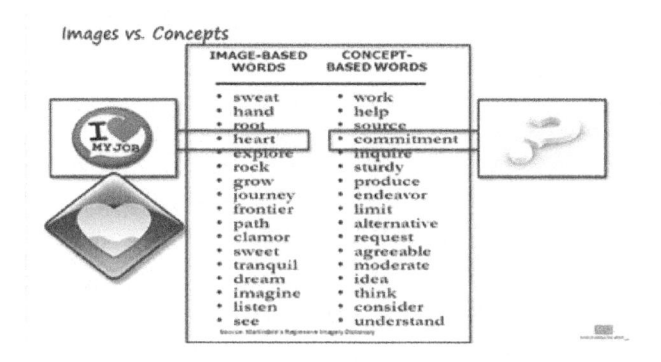

Images vs. Concepts

IMAGE-BASED WORDS	CONCEPT-BASED WORDS
sweat	work
hand	help
root	source
heart	commitment
explore	inquire
rock	sturdy
grow	produce
journey	endeavor
frontier	limit
path	alternative
clamor	request
sweet	agreeable
tranquil	moderate
dream	idea
imagine	think
listen	consider
see	understand

"Image words are stickier. Image words are much more likely to initiate a stronger association/connection. Remember how we learn a language, we connect or associate new things with things we already know. Images give a stronger grounding point to things we know. Image words are far more powerful than concept words. They can also provoke emotions.

"Can you imagine if Martin Luther King said, 'I have an idea'?"

"I have a DREAM!"
NOT
"I have an idea."

She showed the slide of Martin Luther King Jr. "No, he said, '*I have a dream!*" Let's look at some great examples of imagery and image words over concept words."

She advanced to the next slide. "I love this imagery by Doctor King.

> **Image example**
> "And we must never forget this as a nation: there are no gradations of the image of God. Every man from treble white to bass black is significant on God's keyboard, precisely because every man is made in the image of God."
>
> Dr. Martin Luther King Jr.
>
> July 4, 1965 Ebenezer Baptist Church Atlanta, Georgia

"Another place to see the use of great imagery is the book of Proverbs by Solomon. Here are some examples comparing typical statements with concepts on the left and imagery statements on the right.

Typical Messages	Message with Images
Things gained improperly produce negative results.	Ill gotten gain may taste sweet, but it turns to gravel in your mouth.
Laziness has many excuses and many fears.	The sluggard says, "There's a lion outside! I'll be killed in the street!"
Intelligent and strong people working together will strengthen each other.	As iron sharpens iron, so one person sharpens another.

"There is some bad news that accompanies images, however," she waited a couple moments for them to process what they thought the bad news might be, then continued, "the more education we have, the more likely we are to speak in . . . " She waited for them to fill their verbal responses. She repeated, "The more likely we are to speak in concepts."

"*Concepts* might indeed be the lingua franca of academics, but *images* are the currency of effective communicators."

Christa walked to the laptop and advanced the slide.

"Continuing our discussion of nine weeping widows, we looked at facts and images. Now let's look at the most powerful of these three attributes: stories."

Stories

"We probably need to sketch out some definition, brush in a little color, and put up some guardrails on what we mean by stories."

She showed the following image. "Let's start with a question. How long is the typical television commercial?"

The group responded with "One minute." "Fifteen seconds." "Thirty seconds." and "Too long." There were verbal and nonverbal affirmations for the last comment.

Christa continued with a smile, "The average TV commercial is about thirty seconds. Why is this relevant to us?" She paused. "I don't know if Madison Avenue knows something about our brains or our brains are conditioned by Madison Avenue, but it turns out that a great story, in the context of what we do, is about thirty seconds. Great storytellers can certainly be effective with longer stories. Still, think of it this way, after thirty seconds, the ice we are standing on gets thinner and thinner. There is some magic in the thirty-second business story."

She changed the image again. "Let's look at a way to build this thirty-second story."

1. The Window of Attention
2. Conflict
3. Conflict resolution / Climax
4. Facts
5. Images
6. Hero of the Story
7. Voice Zoom

"We already discussed the *window of attention*, which we said was . . ."

The participants responded with "thirty seconds."

"Next, every good story has to have conflict. Then there needs to be a resolution of the *conflict* or a *climax*. In our context, this *climax* or *conflict resolution* isn't something like a super hero movie. It usually has a much softer landing."

She pointed to number four. "Good stories usually have germane *facts*. They also need *images*. Just a little while ago, we discussed the difference between image words and concept words."

She looked out over most of the audience before she posed her next question. "What is the sixth step here?"

The group responded accurately, "The hero of the story."

"Based upon what we have covered today—particularly in terms of the focus of our communications—who should be the hero of our stories?" She paused.

The participants hesitated and then began offering their thoughts, "It depends." "Not me." "Not us." "The folks we are talking to." "Our customers." "Our colleagues." "Anybody but us."

Christa nodded approvingly. "You got it. The inherent danger and our natural tendency is to make ourselves the *hero* of the story. *That* is exactly the wrong thing to do. We need to make others, our clients and colleagues, the hero of our stories."

"Last on this list of story elements is this strange term *voice zoom*. We will hold on discussing this for a moment.

"An example might help. One of my clients shared this with me. He was doing consulting work for a large computer company, which underwent some troublesome times. They were rudderless because they were without a CEO for almost a year. They finally got a new CEO, and they wanted to communicate to the market that they were again going to be a vibrant lead player in the market.

"I will share the messaging they used in two fashions: one without a story and the other through a story.

"Here is the first messaging approach that was used with customers and the market." She turned to the right side of the audience in an obvious role play mode.

"We have a new CEO, he is a person of action, he really cares about customers, and he is really going to make a difference."

She moved out of her role play. "So how sticky was that? How sticky was that messaging?"

The group was unenthusiastic. "Not very sticky, weak, corporate speak."

"Agreed." She asked another question, "How typical is that kind of messaging?"

The group was very affirmative. "Typical, classic stuff, same-old corporate speak."

"Let me give you the same message in a different way." She turned to the left side of the audience and again stepped into a role play.

"We have a new CEO. He was on the job for four hours. He got on the company's corporate jet and flew to our biggest customer. He sat down with them and he said, 'Tell me what we are doing well, but most importantly, tell me what we need to change?'"

"Which of the two messaging approaches was stickier?"

With unanimity, the group responded, "The story."

She pointed to her watch and asked, "How long was the story?"

There were multiple guesses.

"Depending on my pace today, it took between 13 to 17 seconds to tell, way under thirty seconds." She pointed to seven elements of the story on the screen, then said, "Let's dissect the story.

"How long was it?"

They responded with "Well under thirty seconds."

"What was the conflict?"

From a variety of voices, "No CEO." "No direction." "No leader."

"What was the conflict resolution?"

As one voice, "A new CEO. A new leader."

"What were the facts?"

The audience paused momentarily, then said, "Four hours." "Largest customer." "Company jet."

"What were the images?"

Some responded dispassionately, "Corporate jet." "The jet thing." Some with disdain. "Private jet."

Christa smiled at the differences in responses. "For some, particularly those who have not worked for big companies, the corporate jet image sets their hair on fire. Others are okay with it because they know that every big company uses corporate jets. It is a controversial image. I leave it in the story for two reasons. One, it is germane to the story. It would be nearly impossible to have the required door-to-door speed flying commercially. Two, it is a good reminder that images are powerful, but they can also engender negative associations/connections.

"Who was the hero?"

Unanimously. "The CEO."

"Great, any questions on the first six elements?"

She waited, but there were no questions, so she continued, "Now let's talk about voice zoom. We invented this strange label, but many people naturally use this approach. You will see that great storytellers naturally use voice zoom all the time."

She walked over to her laptop but did not advance the slide. "I know that some of you were probably English majors in college and are perhaps experts in grammar. Tell me the difference between using the third person and the first person."

A smartly dressed older woman in the seventh row on the left raised her hand and spoke, "There is the first person, *I*, the second person, *you*, and the third person, *he*, *she*, or *it*. If someone is using the third person, they might say something like, '**She threw the marker at the young man without warning and almost killed him.**'"

The woman who answered the question received enthusiastic support from her workshop colleagues for poking fun at Christa.

The woman waited for the side comments to subside, and then continued, "If one were to convert the statement to the first person, it might be, '**I almost killed someone today with a marker.**'"

Christa smiled. "Perfect. Now let's see how this played out in the story I shared."

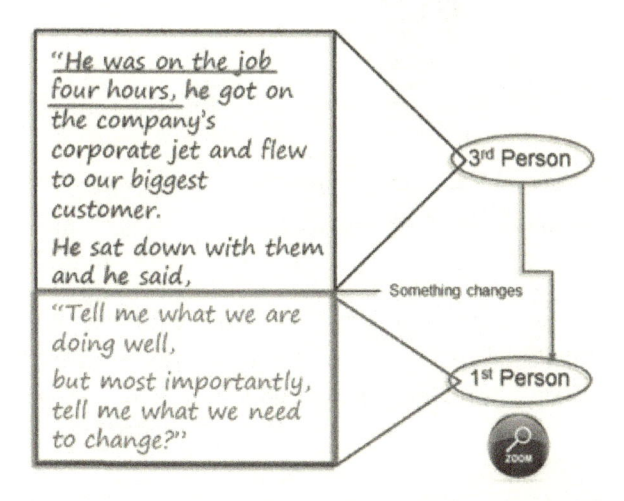

> "He was on the job four hours, he got on the company's corporate jet and flew to our biggest customer. — 3rd Person
>
> He sat down with them and he said,
>
> — Something changes
>
> "Tell me what we are doing well, but most importantly, tell me what we need to change?" — 1st Person
>
> ZOOM

She advanced the slide. "'*He was on the job four hours*'—this is in the third person. Then it morphs into the first person—into a role play—'*tell me what we are doing well, but most importantly what do we need to change?*' Notice how this changing of voice just brings us right into the room. It zooms you in closer to the action—that is why we call it voice zoom. Again, as I said, good storytellers do this all of the time.

"So this is nine weeping widows. The use of facts, images, and stories. Every political speech, every State of the Union Address, every message from the pulpit—whether rabbi, priest, minister, or imam—regularly uses these three elements. We need to make facts, images, and stories an essential part of our standard communications." Then she advanced the slide.

Christa gave the group ten minutes to write a thirty-second story, and then the group discussed five of them.

"We have covered a lot of ground this morning. Thank you for being so wonderfully engaged. It is time for lunch and the wonderful spread the folks here at Babson provide. Enjoy! I will see you in an hour."

Christa checked her phone. There were no voicemails or text messages, nor did she receive any during the lunch break. She was looking forward to a response from her dad.

Chapter 7

Banners

"Thank you for your prompt return from lunch." There was a refreshed tone in her voice and an increased quickness in her step. "How was lunch?" There was applause. "They never disappoint here." With a knowing smile, she said, "My guess is that, perhaps, a few of you have a couple extra desserts stuffed in a pocket or purse." There were several head nods of affirmation.

She transitioned and advanced the slide.

"Let's talk about banners. What the heck are banners?" She paused. "Before we define what we mean by banners, let me ask you a question. Earlier today, we discussed the difference between concept words and image words. Is the word *message* a concept word or an image word?"

Most of the participants said, "Concept word."

She surveyed the room. "Correct. It is a concept word, and as we agreed, we want to use image words. So let's walk the talk here. Let's focus on images. Let's look at understanding the stickiness of our messages by calibrating the stickiness of banners."

She advanced to the next slide. "Let's define banners. Imagine you are having either an internal meeting with colleagues or an external meeting with clients or prospects. Picture each person in the meeting going back to their office or cube after the meeting and putting up a small banner, characterizing what they took away from the meeting. They might have walked away with any of the following:

This was a waste of my time.

It was all about them; they didn't address a single concern of mine.

Interesting. I need to think about this more.

Thoughtful and great understanding of the problem. Could work.

On the money.

Let's get started.

The Gift of Silence

Banners: A Visual Way To Calibrate Stickiness

After the meeting, each meeting participant goes back to their office. They each put up a 'Banner' about you...

What would it say?

- This was a waste of my time
- It was 'all about them', they didn't address a single concern of mine.
- Interesting. I need to think on this more.
- Thoughtful & great understanding of the problem. Could work.
- On the money. Let's get started

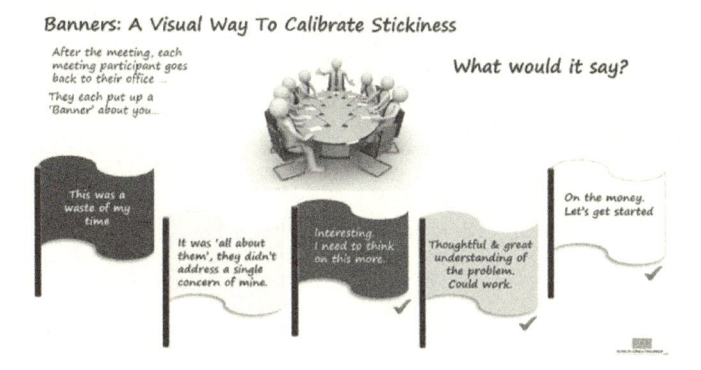

"Which of these banners might we hope to have planted?"

The audience responded, "The ones with check marks." "The ones from middle to right." "The last one."

"Yes, the first two banners are obviously a problem. We would have missed the mark if they walked away with those banners. Obviously, the last one would be the best.

"You can see how banners can help us calibrate how sticky our key messages are. We can use this approach of banners before a meeting and ask ourselves, **'What banners do we want to plant for this meeting?'** In the meeting, we can calibrate by asking, **'How are we doing? What banners are sticking?'** Finally, after the meeting, we can ask ourselves, **'What banners did they walk away with from this meeting?'**

"Banners are an incredibly simple image and an approach to messaging that greatly improves our accuracy in calibrating our messages: Which messages have landed? What messages, intended and unintended messages, stuck both intended?

"What questions do you have about banners?"

Jon, the young man to whom she threw the marker, raised his hand. "How do you know you are accurate in calibrating their takeaways or banners?"

Christa unexpectedly jerked her arm toward her laptop table like she was reaching for a gun in a gunfight and grabbed a marker. Jon feigned, ducking under the table. They both enjoyed the jest.

Christa smiled at him. "Jon, how do you do it now? How do you calibrate what sticks now?"

Jon was stymied a bit by the question. "I probably guess . . . and as you say that . . . I am realizing that I probably don't calibrate stickiness enough. I probably should be asking myself what stuck often more."

An older man, Phil, sitting next to Jon piped in, "I agree with Jon. One of my takeaways from this discussion is that, most of the time, I just make assumptions about what messages people got. I don't usually ask myself what impressions they walk away with."

There were many affirmative nods in the workshop group.

Christa smiled as she watched many of the participants experience this epiphany. "Complexity is the enemy of compliance.

"Banners create such a simple way to practice our art of calibrating stickiness. Banners easily enable us to turn message assessment into a habit. What is especially cool about this assessment approach is when it becomes a group habit. It becomes a group or organizational habit when teams ask themselves before every presentation, **'What banners do we want to plant?'** And after every meeting, **'What banners did they walk after with?'** This raises the level of art for the whole team. This raises the power and the accuracy of our antennae as individuals and as a group.

"Thank you for your questions and comments. Are there any questions about banners?"

Structure

"Let's shift gears a bit to discuss the structure of how we present. Not to oversimplify it, but from my observations, folks present with one or two structures when sharing the information."

She advanced the slide to the following image.

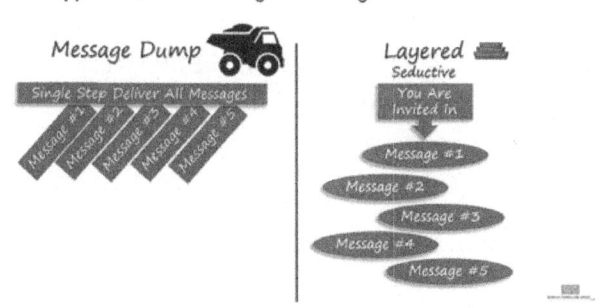

Two Approaches To Delivering Our Messages

Message Dump — Single Step Deliver All Messages (Message #1, Message #2, Message #3, Message #4, Message #5)

Layered — Seductive — You Are Invited In → Message #1 → Message #2 → Message #3 → Message #4 → Message #5

"Folks either use the dump truck structure or the layered structure to their messaging and information.

"The most common approach, by far, is the dump truck structure. Here is how the dump truck structure typically works. We have eighteen things to share, so we roll up the slide deck, dump out all eighteen things, and then, without taking a breath, we shovel, point after point, into the audience's lap. Net-net, we have eighteen things to tell you, and by golly, we are going to line them and deliver them. We get in a tell mode, and we tell number one, then we tell number two, and so on."

Christa walked up to the front of the room again. "How many times have you sat through a presentation like that?"

There were many affirmative responses from the audience.

"As an audience participant in those meetings, how does it feel?" She pointed to a hand that was up.

Eric, a tall, thin man in his thirties on the left, shared, "It sucks. It makes me feel passive."

Christa moved closer to him. "Tell me why it makes you passive, Eric?"

He shrugged his shoulders, clearly unsure of his answer.

Christa moved the spotlight from Eric to make him feel more comfortable. She asked the group, "Eric made a great point, why do all think the dump truck structure makes us passive?"

There were several individual comments from different parts of the room. Finally, a man in the last row raised his hand. Christa acknowledged him. He said passionately, "It comes back to two things we discussed. The dump truck approach makes us feel passive as an audience because there is no space for us to engage. That is what you tried to drive home with the gift of silence. The dump truck approach also screams of what you cautioned that we need to get out of the carpet—'it's all about me'!"

The audience responded with spontaneous applause. Comments were added. "Well done." "Cool." "Bravo."

Christa let him soak in the recognition.

She leaned forward to see the name on his tent card. "It is Tim?"

He nodded.

She smiled at him. "Yes, well said—perfectly said, Tim." She turned to the rest of the group. "Tim is not a plant. There are no campaign trail tactics here."

She drove the conversation to the next step. "So Tim beautifully painted a picture of the downside of the dump truck structure. One of the challenges of examining communication approaches is, it is *easy* to critique but *difficult* to create."

She paused. "What is a better way to structure the information of the presentation?"

The audience easily recognized the answer was on the slide before them; they said, *"Layered."*

Christa grinned. "What do you think that layered means?" She gave the gift of silence.

Someone from behind Jon shouted, "We should probably ask Tim." There was some laughter. Tim waved off the attention and shook his head no.

After a few, moderately accurate attempts at defining layered, someone shouted out, "We are ready to catch the marker, Christa. Why don't you tell us the answer?"

Taking the good-natured coaching, Christa proceeded to explain, "A situation that captures the essence of these contrasting structures is when we are asked the question, **'What do you guys do?'"**

"How many of you have been asked that question about your team or organization at some point?"

Almost everyone's hand went up.

"There are two ways this question typically gets answered, with the dump truck structure or the layered structure.

"If we answer with the dump truck, we back up the truck and give them a long answer, telling them twenty-three things about the organization, of which probably two things are interesting or relevant to them.

"In contrast, if we take the layer, the answer to the question **'What do you guys do?'** we give an incredibly short but respectful answer. It might be a five-second answer. Our answer provides appropriate information, but it also invites questions. We don't share everything we know. We have the discipline and the restraint to invite their questions and their curiosity.

"What does this do?"

A woman on the left offered, "It creates a conversation or a dialogue."

Christa pointed at her appreciatively. "Bingo." Looking at her name card, she said, "Well done, Shevani. What else does this layered structure do?"

Madison in the fifth row on the right volunteered. "It drives the conversation to the things that are important to the person listening and not the twenty-three things that are important to the person speaking."

Christa nodded. "Bingo, yes, on the money, Madison." She surveyed the group. "How clear is the contrast between the dump truck and the layered structure?"

The Gift of Silence

Harrison, who was in the second row on the right and quite close to her, offered, "I get layering in a one-on-one setting, but it is not clear to me how you would do it if you were presenting to a group."

Christa could see that most of the room did not hear his comment. She turned to him and said, "Thank you for the comment, may I impose upon you to repeat it loudly so everyone can hear it and benefit from the comment, Harrison."

Harrison repeated his comment loudly. Many nods affirmed that he had hit a chord with his colleagues.

"So let's answer this." Extending her arms to the group, she asked, "May I have your permission for a moment to be marginally offensive?"

All heads nodded. There were side comments also. "You have our permission. You can be really offensive if you want."

Christa continued, "A few years ago, a CEO said to me, 'You know, Christa, this communication stuff amazes me, not to oversimplify it, but our team should have learned most of what they needed to know about external and internal communication by sitting at the bar and trying to get dates.'"

Christa waited for this idea to wash over the group.

"The CEO had a great point. I have found myself thinking over and over again how some of the common mistakes we make in internal and external communications we would never make at the bar trying to get a date." She counted to three, then continued explaining, "Let's take dump truck messaging and layered messaging as an example. Could you imagine sitting down next to an attractive person you would like to date and saying,

> **let me give you a quick summary of the last twenty-three relationships I have been,**
>
> **let me tell you how I typically like to treat folks on a date,**
>
> **let me list for you the benefits you will experience by dating me, and**
>
> **let me summarize by explaining why I am a great catch?"**

Laughter followed. Some enjoyed the incongruity of the dating image and messaging, and some relished in the indictment of the mistakes we all make.

As the laughter subsided, Christa said, "My apologies for the horrifying flashbacks of bad dates this might cause for you."

She smiled and waited for the chuckles and the sidebars to subside. "Back to layered messaging. Whether in individual conversations or a group, we don't want to lay out the twenty-three last relationships we had. We need to look at the information and determine at which point *we* or *they* have earned the right to discuss those things. I am sure that you see this all the time in work settings, where information is presented and it feels like the cart is put before the horse or that folks have not earned the right to go there. That is one group layering problem.

"The other part of this structure or layering problem is, frankly, just bad technique and a lack of discipline. What do I mean by that?

"The dump truck structure says to the audience that we are going to run down the path and tell, tell, tell. It says that we will identify all the signposts at each point along the way.

"The layered structure says to the audience that we are going to run, but we are going to stop for questions. As matter of fact, at point A, we are going to ask this question of the group, and point B, we are to ask this question of the group. We engage the audience in some of the navigation. Our questions either bring us into a discussion about red or black depending on the interest of the audience.

"The layered structure also carries with it the discipline of 'wait for it.' What do I mean by that?

"This is the discipline of not initiating every topic, but rather anticipating that a question on a topic might be posed, and then addressing the topic at the time the question is posed.

"Let's look at how this has happened twice today.

"When we opened this morning, I posed some questions." Christa smiled at Marissa, who asked the question about the slides. "Which question did you pose to me?"

"I asked you if we could get the slides." Marissa smiled back.

"What percentage of the time do you think I get that question from the group?"

The group thought about it but did not answer.

"About 90 percent of the time. I purposely don't mention it, because I want to wait for the question. Why do I want to wait for the question?"

She counted, then said, "Because your questions create a healthy dialogue early. Also, if I go the whole day without someone asking for the material, it probably means the material and I sucked!"

Christa turned to Helen. "This morning you posed a question about whether or not we should share our message even when we sense folks are not ready." Christa nodded to XYZ, who had posed the question. "How often do you think I get that question?"

The group responded, "90 percent of the time."

Christa smiled. "Sorry, I am not trying to make this a guessing game. I get it about 60 percent of the time. There are a couple reasons I wait for someone to bring up the subject: It is a way for me to manage being on schedule. It is one of several topics, which are important but not essential. I only cover them when asked.

"The other reason is personal. Frankly, I get nervous telling the story about my brother. I won't tell it unless I feel safe and comfortable with the group. Many times, I will just pass on the story."

She gave the group a subtle nod. "Thanks for making me feel safe today.

"Layering is a way to unfold the story we are telling with our messaging. We should think of layering as writing a miniseries, which peels the story a layer at a time and draws folks in with each episode."

Christa looked at Harrison, who had the original point, "Did I answer your question?"

Harrison nodded yes.

Adaptability

Christa advanced to the next slide.

How Often Does This Happen?

You are told you have this amount of time to present...

You actually have this amount of time to present...

"How many of you have had this happen? You are told that you have, say, thirty minutes to present something, and then the meeting starts, and key people say, 'I need to leave in ten minutes for another meeting'?"

She waited for hands from the audience. Almost every hand in the room went up.

"This is obviously a common and consistent problem, so how do we solve this?"

The group offered suggestions: "Shorten our presentations." "Confirm timeframes before we show up." "Go with the flow." "Shame them into staying longer."

"Okay, some good suggestions. We should confirm timeframes, etc. We should try and keep our presentations tight. But let's talk about the secret to enabling us to be adaptable because whatever we do to preclude the problem, it will happen, folks will shorten our time." She walked to the middle of the room. "Has anyone here ever run out of gas or perhaps almost run out of gas in their car?" Most hands went up. "When is the best time to solve the problem of running out of gas?"

Almost unanimously the group contributed, "Before it happens."

"Yes. Absolutely. The best time to solve the problem of running out of gas is before it happens not after it happens. The same is true of getting our presentations shortened. We can do some things to improve the odds that folks won't shorten our presentations, but we all know that no matter what we do, it will happen! So we need to be prepared before it happens. We need to take specific steps so that when it happens we can still be effective." She paused.

"What are those specific steps? What are the specific things we need to do with every presentation?" She surveyed the room to see if participants were trying to discern the answer.

"Let me come back to the question in a few moments, but first, let me give you a specific scenario." She transitioned into an example.

"One stop on my career journey, I worked for a large technology company. In one role, I was responsible for rolling out a new set of technologies. We decided that one thing we would do to introduce the new technologies is to hold breakfasts for customers and prospects in twenty-five cities around the country. We held these at good-sized hotels and averaged a little over 250 attendees in each city.

"We would serve breakfast, have a customer—typically a CTO or CIO talk—and then present our new technologies for forty-five minutes. I would get—from corporate—a new expert presenter on the technologies every fourth city.

"I would go through the same drill with each new presenter. They would arrive in the late afternoon, and we would meet at the hotel. They would take me through their forty-five-minute presentation on their technology. After they were done, I would ask them a few questions. 'Where are you on the agenda tomorrow?' They would say, 'After the customer.'

"Right. How often do you think this customer gets to speak to 250 people?"

"'Probably not very often.'

"Right. What are the chances they will end on time?"

"'Not good.'

"Right. What are the chances that I will get on stage and give them the hook when they go over their time?"

"'Not good.'

"None. Since we are absolutely going to end the breakfast on time, what are the chances that you are actually going to have forty-five minutes to present tomorrow?"

"'Not good.'

"Right. So go up to your hotel room and put together two new presentations. Create a presentation you would use if you only had twenty minutes. Create a presentation you would use if you only had ten minutes. Let's reconvene in a couple hours and go through them."

Christa turned to the Babson audience. "How often do you think we used these shortened presentations?"

They responded, "Lots." "All the time."

She continued, "About 70 percent of the time. What did the exercise force the presenter to do?"

A voice from the back said, "Shorten it."

She nodded. "Indeed. Shortening was the result." She walked over to her laptop and advanced the slide.

She stepped forward again. "For the presenter to shorten their presentation, they had to make foreground and background decisions. They had to decide what were the most important things, and what was background material or supporting material. This is the secret to adaptability.

"Before we ever step up to present our presentation or our messages, we need to specifically identify what is essential—what is the foreground material. Then we can decide what the background material is.

"Do you see how this also complements what we discussed in terms of layering information and messages?"

There were many affirmative nods in the audience.

The Gift of Silence

"Some of you might have heard of Edwin Tufte. He was a longtime professor at Yale and pioneer in the field of data visualization. He talks about avoiding the 'flat land,' where all the information is on the same plane. We need to take our messages, our information, and our presentations, and create mountains, valleys, and plains. We need to layer it to make the material inviting. We need to consciously identify the foreground and background to enable us to be adaptable.

"It's time for a break. Let's take fifteen minutes."

Christa checked her phone. There were no text messages or voicemails. She turned off her phone.

About ten minutes later, while she was speaking to the group, she missed a text from her brother. "Sis, when was the last time you spoke to Dad?"

Chapter 8

The Why, Impact Scale, and "At Stake"

She spoke exactly as the fifteen-minute break concluded, "Thank you for your prompt return from the break. It is greatly appreciated.

"We are going to cover three topics together, which probably deserve a whole day of attention, but given our limitations, we are only going to lay the foundation of this skyscraper today."

She stepped one step to the left. "Besides our time today, think about two internal or external meetings you have sat in recently where you were the receiver of the messages and information. What was the focus? **Was the focus on *how* to do things or on *why* we should do something?**"

She gave the gift of silence.

The group offered a variety of answers, "Both." "How." "Some why, lots of how"

"If you were blessed with an accomplished speaker or presenter, you might have heard some 'why.' But it is most likely you heard a great deal of 'how.'

If you sat through a sales presentation, there was a 97 percent chance that you heard *how* the vendor does things or *why* things should be done.

"If you sat through an internal presentation, you had a very good chance that you heard how we can improve something and very little why we should make the changes."

She let the "how" and "why" pictures formulate in their minds. "Why is this discussion about *the why* and *the how* so important?"

The group offered several different opinions:

> "The how is where most people feel comfortable."

> "The how is where stuff gets done."

> "The how can make us ignore the why."

> "The how is the way to get somewhere, but the why is the destination."

> "The why is what drives change."

She brought them back to question. "Some great points. Again, the question was, Why is a discussion about the 'why' and the 'how' so important?"

"Let's start at the beginning. Why are you all here today?" She saw some knowing smiles. "We are all here today to be more effective communicators, either with colleagues or clients or prospects. That is our why.

"The evidence of being a more effective communicator is our improved ability to move people to actions that are in their best interests."

"How do we improve the odds that folks will want to take action?" She counted before saying, "By connecting them to a why, which is in their own best interest."

"Sounds easy. But here is the problem. The natural pull of gravity in the physics of messaging is how not why. For some reason—whether we are left-brained or not—we gravitate toward 'how *does* it work?'

"We focus on the how versus why. Sales messaging is the worst offender." She paused. "The irony is that although the gravity-pull and the natural play is the how the impetus to action comes from the why."

"Remember this morning, we talked about looking at each of our messages and asking, 'Who is this about, me or them?' We need to make similar self-assessments in looking at our messaging and asking, 'In addition to the how stuff, have we driven home the why?'"

She folded her hands gently behind her back. "What are your thoughts on this?"

There was a lively exchange between the participants. Some understood exactly what she was saying, and others struggled with the idea that there was too much focus on the how.

"Great exchange. Thank you. Forgive me for not being very clear. When you don't understand something, it is my fault." She paused. "How many of you have been involved in a commercial buying process in the last six months where either you were a part of a team making a purchasing decision for your company or you were part of a team proposing to a company to purchase something from you or someone else?"

Approximately, 80 percent of the hands in the room went up.

"Now think through the related conversations, what percentage of those conversations were focused on how stuff works versus why are we doing this?"

Responses came from all over the room, "80 percent." "Almost 100 percent." "90 percent."

"Very simply, that is the natural gravitational pull of the how. This is the reason ideas, projects, initiatives get stuck in the mud all the time because the focus is on the how, but the impetus comes from the why."

There were many affirmative nods.

"So how do we defy gravity? How do we shift the conversation to the why? Let me give you one approach for consideration."

Impact

"One way to change the focus from the how to the why is to move the conversation to the *impact*. We can do this by asking the folks impact questions like these: 'What impact do you think this will have on the organization?' 'If we do XYZ, what impact do you think this will have?' In a sales situation, we might ask, 'Whether you do this with us or someone else, what do you think the impact will be?'

"These impact questions are only the first step. They bring us closer to the why. But they typically don't get us where we need to be because the answers to these questions are usually too thin. Remember, most people are unaccustomed to thinking in the why, so when we bring them into the why territory, they typically don't know how to navigate to the mountain tops.

"How do we solve this? Let's look at a map that might help us scale the mountain. We call it the impact scale. Here is a snapshot of the impact scale.

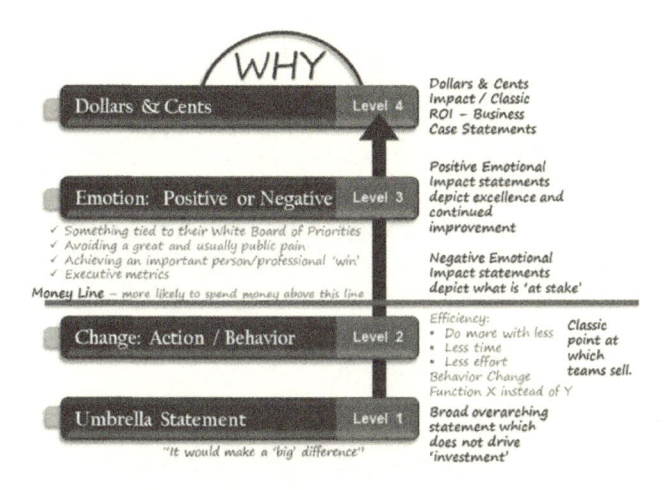

WHY

Dollars & Cents	Level 4	Dollars & Cents Impact / Classic ROI – Business Case Statements
Emotion: Positive or Negative	Level 3	Positive Emotional Impact statements depict excellence and continued improvement

✓ Something tied to their White Board of Priorities
✓ Avoiding a great and usually public pain
✓ Achieving an important person/professional 'win'
✓ Executive metrics

Negative Emotional Impact statements depict what is 'at stake'

Money Line – more likely to spend money above this line

Change: Action / Behavior	Level 2	Efficiency: • Do more with less • Less time • Less effort Behavior Change Function X instead of Y — Classic point at which teams sell.
Umbrella Statement	Level 1	Broad overarching statement which does not drive 'investment'

"It would make a 'big' difference"

"When we ask an impact question, like **'What impact do you think this will have on the organization?'** we are likely to get a low-level answer—an answer that leaves us at the foot of the mountain. We will hear things like **'It would make a difference.'** *'It would really help.' 'It would be great.'*

"These are umbrella statements. They are broad, powder-puff impact statements lacking gravitas. They are level one impact statements. These statements do not provide enough impetus to action.

"We might also hear a stronger answer to the impact question—they might make level two Impact statements—like **'We will take less time.' 'It will be more efficient.' 'We will use fewer resources.'**

"Level two impacts are change statements. Something works a certain way now, but afterward, it will work differently. Level two impacts tend to focus on efficiency in depicting change: it will be faster, take less time, or take less effort. Instead of behaving like X, it will behave like Y.

"Two problems make the level two impact statement weak and ineffectual. First, level two statements rarely pass the 'so what' test:

> 'All right, we make this change, so what?'
> 'All right, it is faster, so what?'
> 'All right, it makes us more efficient, so what?'

"Second, look at where level two statements sit. Look at the line above level two. What is it?"

The group responded, "The money line."

"Bingo. The money line is where organizations are likely to invest money or resources. By the way, most sales teams message at level two—change statements. This is one of the reasons so many sales campaigns get stuck.

"So let's talk about where there is the real impetus. Let's look at where we really start to scale the mountain of why. This happens at level three and level four impact statements.

"Level three and level four impact statements are of equal weight. They both provide substantial impetus. I just couldn't figure out a better way to label them.

"Maybe a better way to look at the value of level three and level four impacts is from a simple math point of view. Their value together is *not* three plus four or seven. Rather their value together is more like thirty-four.

"You are all quite familiar with level four impacts—these are dollars-and-cents impacts. They are classically labeled as ROI, return on investment, impacts.

"These dollars-and-cents impacts are important, but beware that ROI and its variants are not the holy grail. Let me say it again, ROI and its variants are not the holy grail. Let me say it a third time, ROI is not the holy grail.

"Too many organizations think if they can just develop a way to demonstrate ROI, they will overcome all obstacles. Nonsense. It is just not that simple. We should not allow our teams to be that naive.

"So where do level three impacts fit? What the heck are these level three impacts? Level three impacts are emotional impacts that are tied to the organization's and the individual's white board of priorities.

"Every organization on the planet has a metaphorical or physical white board of priorities. These are the things the most senior people in the organization discuss when they huddle. These are the 'big rocks.'

"These white board of priorities can be positive things like being first in the market, being viewed as XYZ, being innovative, the ability to adapt, and the ability to develop leaders. These priorities might be something like being seen as the best place for cardiac care in a region. These positive impacts are often identified in the KPIs or OKRs of the leaders of the organization.

"Level three impacts can also be negative. We don't want to be on the front page of the *Wall Street Journal* for X, or we don't want to be the poster child for Z type of problems.

"Level three and level four impacts give teeth to the why. They scale us to the top of the why mountain. As I said earlier, when we can put both level three and level four impact statements together as the why, we create an incredibly powerful impetus for action."

She stopped, looked around the room and calibrated the stickiness of impact statements. "What questions do you have?"

There were no initial questions. She smiled at them. "Great, it is practice time. Professionals practice. I want you to take five minutes and write down one level four impact statement and one level 4 impact statement."

The group worked quietly for five minutes, and then Christa facilitated a discussion and evaluation of seven of the participant's level three and level four examples.

After she felt they sufficiently understood impact statement, she transitioned to the last part of the why discussion: at stake.

"We have been talking about the why. The natural pull and gravity of the how. We looked at the impact scale and specifically level three and level four impact statements an approach to articulating the why with teeth. Now let's talk about real physics."

She smiled as she saw the anticipated confusion caused by her purposeful non sequitur.

"Stay with me a moment. What is Newton's first law?"

An older man in the middle raised his hand and shared, "Inertia."

Christa nodded. "Tim, yes, can you recite it?"

Tim smiled. "If I remember it correctly—from back in ancient time when I took physics—it states, '**A body at rest will remain at rest and a body in motion will remain in motion unless . . .**'" He hesitated. "Can't remember the last part, but it has something to do with **encountering a body.**"

His workshop mates provided strong applause.

Christa clapped as well. "Well done!" She turned to the rest of the group and repeated, "A body at rest will remain at rest. This is the natural order of things. While with our messages, we are trying to move folks to action, what do they naturally want to do?"

"Remain at rest," the audience responded.

"Correct. We drive the focus on the why through level three and level four impact statements, and we, indeed, might be successful many times. But there are also many times where we encounter the nasty villain of Dr. Do Nothing! How many times have you worked on an idea, a project, an initiative, and it got killed by the evil villain Dr. Do Nothing?"

There was unanimous affirmation from the group, "Lots, all the time."

"So what weapon can we use against the evil Dr. Do Nothing? In the warlock movies, what needs to be driven through the heart of an evil vampire?"

"A stake," they responded.

She unobtrusively walked over to her laptop and advanced the slide. "The weapon we can use to kill Dr. Do Nothing is 'at stake.'

"We need to ask ourselves, we need to ask our colleagues, we need to ask our clients, and we need to ask our prospects, 'What is at stake for doing nothing?'"

As she lifted her hand and held up a finger with each of the three points, she said, "These things can help us create the impetus to action with our messaging:

> Recognize the gravitational pull is the how and refocus on the why.
> Identify the level three and level four impacts to provide teeth for the why.
> Kill Dr. Do Nothing by identifying what is at stake for doing nothing."

She lowered her hand. "What questions do you have on the why or anything else we have discussed at this point?"

There were no questions.

"Time for a quick break. I will see you in fifteen minutes."

Chapter 9

"Thank you for your prompt return from the break. We are going to cover a couple short topics in this next section. Let's start with quotes.

"Quotes are a very subtle, but extremely powerful way to improve our communication.

"Nothing says I heard you like a quote." Christa advanced the slide. She continued, "Some of you are probably asking yourself, '**What does she mean by quotes? Is it quotes in written documents? Is it quotes in a presentation? Is it quotes in a conversation?**'"

Nothing Says I Heard You Like QUOTES!

The audience agreed.

"When we think of using quotes, we should consider quotes in all these situations.

"If we are writing an email to a colleague, a superior, a client, or a prospect, and we are affirming their thoughts or direction, what better way to say 'I heard you' to them than with a quote.

"If we are giving a presentation and we going to discuss things that we have discovered are important to the group, what better way to say 'I heard you' to them than with quotes.

"If we are having a conversation and we want to reiterate what the other person said, what better way is there to demonstrate 'I heard you' to them than with a quote."

She gave the gift of silence. She smiled then said, "I know that you have thoughts and questions about this." She motioned with her hand to bring the questions forward.

A man in the second raised his hand.

Christa recognized him with a nod. She read his tent card and said, "It is Paul, correct?"

Paul put his hand down. "Yes, it is. . . I get why we might want to use quotes, but frankly, I see two pretty big problems with this."

Christa nodded. "Okay, what problems?"

Paul continued, "First, it seems a bit unrealistic to think we can actually capture people's exact words, and second, I would think it would piss people off when we quote them."

Christa smiled acceptingly. "Really piss them off?"

The Gift of Silence

Paul replied, "Yeah, really pissed them off."

Christa stepped closer to the audience and Paul. "Thank you for putting the two questions on the table of how can we realistically capture people's exact words and doesn't this piss people off." She extended her arm to the audience. "Who would like to take a shot at answering Paul's excellent questions?"

There was a brief hesitation in the group.

Joel, a man in his forties sitting in the middle right, spoke, "I'll take a shot at it."

Christa gestured for him to continue.

Joel grinned a bit. "May I have your permission to address the second question first?" Joel's sender/receiver question wasn't lost on the audience. He continued when he got Christa's smile as an acceptance. He turned around and faced Paul and directed a question at him, "Paul, did Christa piss you off when she had a little dialogue just now?"

Paul was clearly horrified. "No, why would you say that?'

Joel looked down at his notes and then looked up and back at Paul. "Because by my count, she quoted you three times, and you didn't even know it. First, she used your word **problems**. Second, she then asked you if you meant 'really, **pissed them off**,' and then third, she quoted you when she put your questions to the group to answer. She used your words from both questions: **realistically capture people's exact words and again pissed them off.**"

Christa restrained herself from saying anything; Joel was on a roll.

Joel then addressed Paul's first question, "In terms of it being realistic to capture exact words, I am guessing that we are talking about just what Christa did with you. She captured exactly only the words and phrases, which might be your signature phrases. As an example, '**unrealistically capture exact words**' and '**piss people off**.'" Joel turned, facing completely forward. "Capturing the signature words and phrases makes capturing the quotes **realistic**."

The audience clapped.

Christa turned to Paul. "Did Joel answer your questions?"

Paul nodded and grinned. "Yes, thank you . . . Joel is a plant right?"

The group enjoyed a moment of poking fun at Christa. Then she asked, "What other questions do you have about using quotes?"

A woman in a gray business suit on the right asked, "What practical tips do you have for taking notes in a way that makes it easier to capture quotes?"

"Thank you for your question, Joy." Christa again invited the audience to answer with a gesture. "I am sure some of you are already quite good at capturing quotes, would you like to answer Joy's question?"

Maurice, who was on the middle, left spoke, "I am Maurice. I am not a plant."

The group responded with chuckles and some sidebar comments.

Maurice continued, "I had a mentor fifteen years ago that was insistent I capture quotes. He drilled it into me, and it stuck. One thing that has worked great for me is to assign space on the page just for quotes. As an

The Gift of Silence

example, if I am taking notes on a legal pad, I only write quotes in the left-hand margin—I use about a third of the page on the left. It makes it very easy to find the quotes later.

"Sometimes, I also use my Surface and OneNote to take notes. I circle all the quotes with red color because it is fast and easy to change the pen color on the electronic pen in OneNote.

"One other thing, Joel's point about signature words and phrases is absolutely gold. I couldn't do this quote thing until I figured out I had to listen for the most important words and phrases and *not* everything. I love the label he gave, calling it **signature words and phrases**."

Someone sitting three rows below him asked Maurice, "Do you ask permission to take notes?"

Maurice looked at Christa for direction about whether he or she should answer the question; Christa deferred to Maurice.

Maurice responded, "I was taught that if you are in person with someone, you should ask permission to take notes because notetaking can break eye contact and you don't want to appear rude or inattentive. I also ask permission on the phone when I think the material might be very sensitive and they might not want me to take notes."

Christa gave two thumbs-up to Maurice.

The group discussion continued for about three minutes. There were a couple of other suggestions around Post-it Notes and using multicolor ink pens.

Christa wrapped up the section. "Any other comments or questions?" She paused. "Net-net, try using quotes if you don't use quotes today. You will find it absolutely improves listening and improves the stickiness of what we say because we are using their words . . . to quote Joel—their signature words. Nothing says we heard you like a quote."

The Standard Presentation Deck

Christa moved into the next short topic. "How many of you have a standard presentation or a standard deck, which your teams present to customers and prospects?"

Almost everyone's hand went up.

"In the spirit of improving our communications and at the risk of offending you or your organizations, let's discuss the standard deck or standard presentation. There is nothing intrinsically wrong with having a standard deck or standard presentation. A standard deck can actually be a very good thing. The real question is, How is the standard deck used?

"Before we drill down on that, let me ask a question. **What is the difference between a monologue and a dialogue?**"

Phil in the fourth row offered definitions, "A monologue is one person talking. Dialogue is an exchange between one or more people."

Christa gave him a thumbs-up and advanced to the following slide.

monologue

[ˈmänəlˌôg, ˈmänəlˌäg]
NOUN
1. a long speech by one actor in a play or movie, or as part of a theatrical or broadcast program.
2. "he was reciting some of the great monologues of Shakespeare" · [more]
3. *synonyms*:
4. soliloquy · speech · address · lecture · oration · sermon · homily · dramatic monologue · interior monologue · spiel
5. a long, tedious speech by one person during a conversation.
6. "Fred carried on with his monologue as if I hadn't spoken"

dialogue

[ˈdīəˌlag, ˈdīəˌlôg]
NOUN
1. conversation between two or more people as a feature of a book, play, or movie.
2. "the book consisted of a series of dialogues" · [more]
3. *synonyms*:
4. conversation · talk · communication · interchange · discourse · argument · [more]
VERB
NORTH AMERICAN
1. take part in a conversation or discussion to resolve a problem.
2. "he stated that he wasn't going to dialogue with the guerrillas"

"So how do monologue and dialogue relate to standard presentation decks?"

She gave the gift of silence.

Phil offered again, "We want to have dialogues with people, and we want to avoid monologues."

Christa advanced to the next slide and said, "Absolutely!" She waited for the group to digest the change in the image.

monologue
[mänəl ôg, mänəl äg]
NOUN
1. a long speech by one actor in a play or movie, or as part of a theatrical or broadcast program.
2. "he was reciting some of the great monologues of Shakespeare" · [more]
3. synonyms:
4. soliloquy speech address lecture oration sermon homily dramatic monologue interior monologue spiel
5. a long, tedious speech by one person during a conversation.
6. "Fred carried on with his monologue as if I hadn't spoken"

ALWAYS THE SAME

dialogue
[dīə läg, dīə lôg]
NOUN
1. conversation between two or more people as a feature of a book, play, or movie.
2. "the book consisted of a series of dialogues" [more]
3. synonyms:
4. conversation talk communication interchange discourse argument [more]
VERB
NORTH AMERICAN
1. take part in a conversation or discussion to resolve a problem.
2. "he stated that he wasn't going to dialogue with the guerrillas"

ALWAYS DIFFERENT

"The uncomfortable truth is that if by a standard deck or standard presentation we mean we always give the same presentation, then by definition, we are giving a monologue!"

She stopped to let the group chew on her point.

"If, on the other hand, our standard deck or standard presentation is merely a consistent structure to be filled with different content specific to each audience, then we have a dialogue.

"I see both. I also see the windup doll approach where the subject matter expert or the sales person turns on their deck and lets it roll. After seeing them go through the deck twice, you can almost lip-synch the words. It is a monologue.

"I see folks take the standard deck, and every time they deliver it, it has key different elements that fit like a glove on the audience's hand.

"Net-net, if the presentation is always the same, it is a monologue and a miss. If the standard deck is customized to fit each customer or prospect, it is likely to be an effective dialogue."

Chapter 10

A Model for Presenting

"How many of you have had the privilege or perhaps the pain of sitting through vendor presentations?"

Most of the hands in the group went up.

"In terms of internal presentations, how often are internal presentations excellent presentations?"

Most of the audience gave a thumbs-down or shook their heads from side to side.

"So based upon your experience, is it safe to make this statement: MOST PRESENTATIONS SUCK!" she shouted with a flourish.

Every head nodded.

"Why do most presentations miss the mark?"

The group tossed comment after comment.

"'All about me' problem."

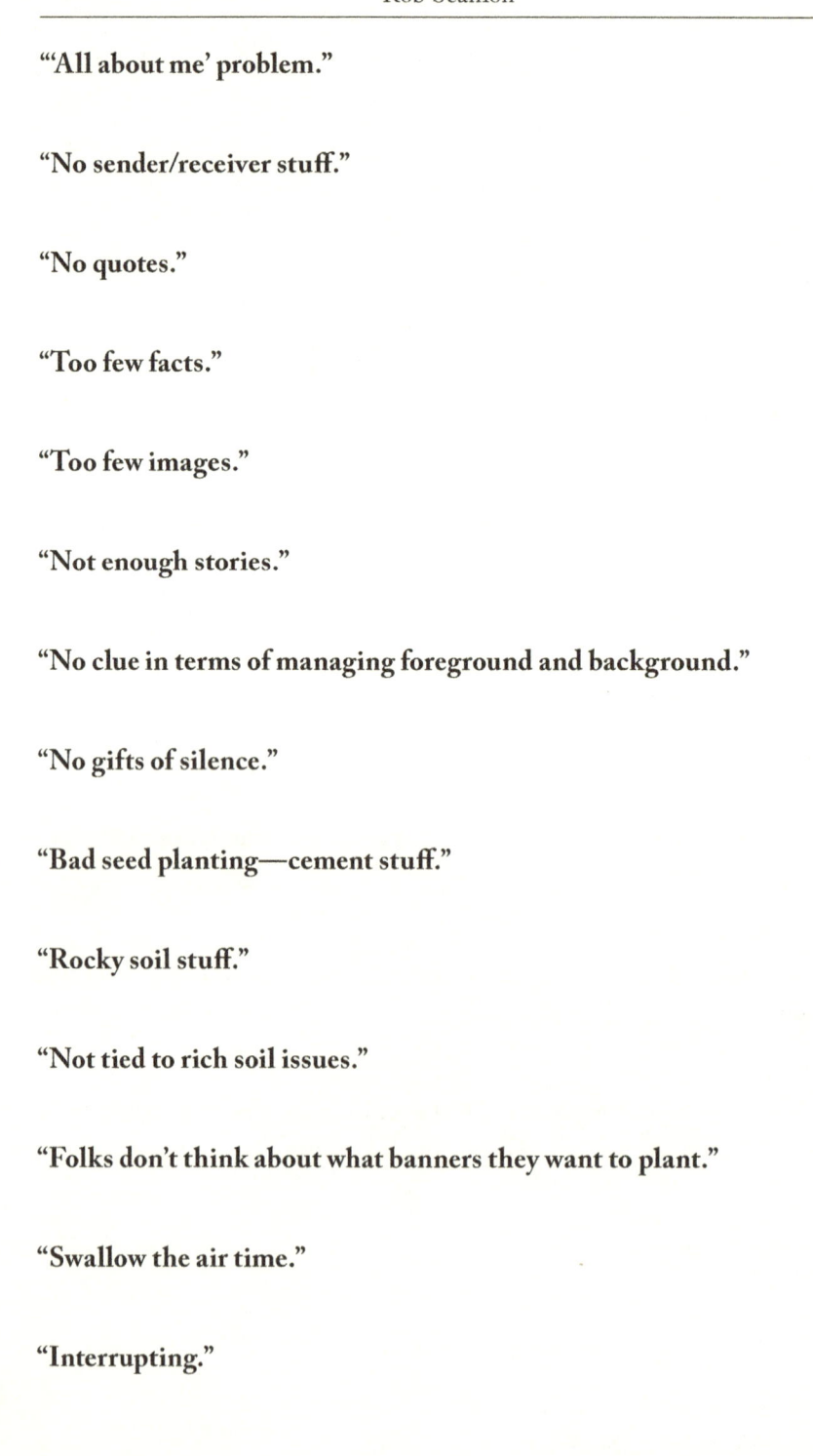

"No sender/receiver stuff."

"No quotes."

"Too few facts."

"Too few images."

"Not enough stories."

"No clue in terms of managing foreground and background."

"No gifts of silence."

"Bad seed planting—cement stuff."

"Rocky soil stuff."

"Not tied to rich soil issues."

"Folks don't think about what banners they want to plant."

"Swallow the air time."

"Interrupting."

"No empathy."

"Not connected to a why."

"Too much how."

"Didn't build trust."

"Didn't demonstrate competence"

"Rolled up the dump truck."

"Didn't layer messages."

"Wow, well done. Thank you. Very impressive." She waited for the compliment to alight.

"There are lots of things we have already discussed that impact the quality of the presentation. We also talked about how most internal and external presentations badly miss the mark. There is a bit of a danger here, and that it is easy to poke fun at things, it is easy to critique. But it is difficult to create a better way.

"Let me show you a different approach, which I think you will find to be a better way. It provides a solid model for applying the long list of things you all just mentioned.

"Before we look at a different model, let's take a look at the current model in vogue today. How do presentations typically start today?"

"With agendas," echoed by many in the group.

"Who creates the agenda?" Christa continued with her questions.

The participants responded, "The presenter." "Sometimes the presenter." "Some from the audience."

"What are classically the first topics discussed?"

The group offered a variety of answers.

"What the presenter wants to accomplish."

"What the presenter sees as the problem."

"Background on the company, if they are presenting to a prospect."

"Background on each of the players who are presenting."

"What the vendor has done for the customer, if presenting to a customer."

"What is the product or solution."

"The logo rodeo slide with all the customer logos in the coral."

Christa smiled. "Excellent as usual. A very thorough list. Who are almost all of these things about the presenters or the audience?"

"The presenters," the group responded as a chorus.

"So the first fatal flaw in a standard presentation is that it starts with a focus on the presenter and not the audience. This greatly increases the odds that the audience will be disconnected or resistant.

"Let me show you a very different presentation model."

Christa advanced the slide.

```
                    'ABOUT THEM'
                    'About the Audience'
Focus of the Discussion
                              'ABOUT US'
                              'About our Solution'
                              'About our Company'
```

Progression of Time During the Presentation

"Notice on the horizontal axis, there is the progression of time in the presentation. The vertical axis is the focus of the discussion.

"Based on what was said earlier, the common approach to internal and external presentations is we start about *us*. This model turns the classic model on its head, and it starts about *them* and morphs into *us* and ends with *them*."

She let the group digest the picture.

"This is an incredibly simple but a markedly different way than most presentations are structured. Let's put some teeth on the model. Let's answer the question, **So how exactly does the model work?**"

She advanced to the next slide.

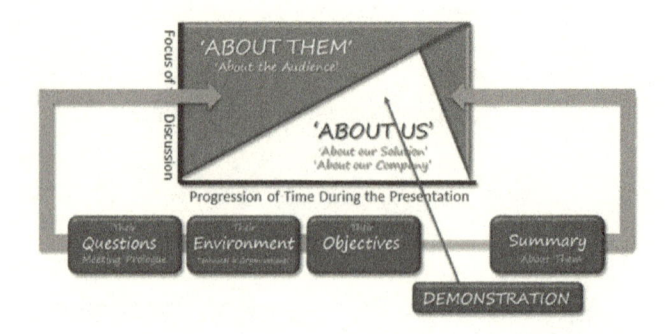

"Here is how we execute the presentation model step-by-step.

"First, we open the meeting with *questions*—the questions we think they want to address.

"Second, we talk a little about their *environment*. This is optional. Sometimes, it makes sense to do a quick check about what we know in terms of their world and what is going on, their process and approaches, and perhaps, key investment strategies they have deployed.

"Third, we identify their *objectives*—the things that they want to accomplish. This is where their quotes can be incredibly powerful.

"Notice that all three of these steps are about whom?"

The participants responded, "About them."

"Yes, because it is about them and not us, you will find that this radically changes the level of interaction at the beginning of the presentation. It really gets the audience talking and engaged.

"After we open with questions, we do a quick check on their environment, identify their objectives, then we can shift into the more common things we do. We can do a demonstration or discuss a reference, if we are doing a prospect or customer presentation. We can discuss our findings or describe our proposal if it is an internal presentation.

"Finally, we want to end the presentation about them. To do that, we go back to their objectives and what they wanted to accomplish.

"Let me stop here for questions."

The group had several questions about what elements might be in the environment and where and when we would use this section.

Christa summarized the discussion about the environment. "The environment section is the least important. It is optional. It works great when we need to confirm some must-be-in-place items for our proposal or solution to be a success. We don't want to devote too much time here.

"I would like to go back and drill a little deeper on the questions and how we open, on the objectives, and on the summary, which takes it back to them. The opening questions we call a meeting prologue.

"Here is the essence of the meeting prologue:

1. We put ourselves in their shoes and determine what we think will be some of the most important things to them.
2. We put these topics into a question format so what we say will be both engaging and focused on them—their questions.
3. We check to see if these in deed are *some* of their questions.
4. We ask if there are any other questions.
5. We check on the time.
6. We answer the questions.

"We do the first step as an exercise in empathy. This changes our headset from us to them.

"We do the second step to keep the focus on their questions.

"We do the third step because this is critical in building a collaborative agenda for the presentation. By the way, it is impossible to get everyone's questions perfectly right, the power here is in our positive intent to understand them. Since we can't get all the questions right, we need to use a critical little phrase: **Are these *some* of your questions?**

"We are moving down the path of collaborating and building a common agenda together.

"In the fourth step, we solicit other questions. This helps us smoke out things we might have missed. It also is another step in building a common agenda together.

"Fifth, we confirm the time we have to present so that we minimize the surprises of participants having to leave early.

"Lastly, we give a short answer to the questions posed.

"Questions?"

The group hesitated. Finally, a woman on the far right, Valerie, asked, "I can see where this could be really great with prospects and customers, can you really do this internally?"

Christa walked to the right and closer to Valerie. "Thank you for the question. The answer is an unequivocal yes!

"I mentioned, earlier in the day, that I had a role in a large technology company related to new product introductions. I had a pretty large group of excellent professionals, and we had many meetings. I made the meeting prologue mandatory for the start of every meeting. When I left the company, they gave me a party and a roast. Everyone roasted me with prologue questions. They were really funny and painful. My favorite person in the group—Luke, who often gave me the hardest time—ended the roast with **'And the final question you probably have is, "Are we going to continue to open every meeting with those stinking questions?" Hell, yes!'**

"Any other questions about starting the meeting with questions?"

Christa walked back to the middle of the room.

"Let's revisit the objectives section. This should be the heart of the presentation. Whether it is external or internal, the objectives set the target. Our messages in the presentation are arrows that need to hit that target. The objectives could be broad big-rock objectives, where, perhaps, our purpose for the day is to provide information, color, context, data, and other things, which help them along the path to bigger objectives. Again, this is a beautiful place to use quotes:

"John, you said you wanted to do X.

"Ann, I think your exact words were 'change our swing so that our team can adjust to the new market.'

"Dr. Jones said, 'Our patients need to get checked in seven minutes and not the twenty-five minutes it takes today so that when I see them, they have smiles rather than having their hair on fire.'

"So the objectives are the target. The logical way to end, the best way to summarize, and the way to bring the discussion back to them is to end with their objectives. We might do this by saying:

> **You said your objectives were XYZ, and that for our time together today, you wanted to get a better understanding of ways to get to XYZ.**

"If we really have courage, we might even end this way:

> **You said your objectives were XYZ, and that for our time together today, you wanted to get a better understanding of ways to get to XYZ. How did we do?"**

Christa could feel that some in the group were very uncomfortable with the question, **How did we do?**

"We need to do things that make sense to us. We need to do things within our own comfort zone. It takes courage to pose the question '**How did we do?**' against their objectives. We won't always like the answer, but we will definitely get a clearer picture of where we stand in terms of landing our messages.

Chapter 11

"We have indeed covered a lot of ground today. You have been very engaged and have asked terrific questions. You probably are wondering **what else in the world could we cover.**

"We have two more laps to go. Two more topics: questions and listening.

"Let me ask you, **Why might we want to make a stop and discuss the art of questions if our mission today is to improve the way we communicate?**"

There were several responses from the group, "Good communicators use questions effectively." "Questions set up our messages." "Questions are tough to master." "Most of us stink at using questions."

Christa nodded affirmatively. She waited for someone to find the epicenter.

Joel offered his thoughts again, "Christa, all day you have been trying to help us get the 'all about me' stuff out of the carpet. You have alluded to the dangers of the tell mode. Questions help us extricate ourselves from the tell mode and the 'all about me' mode into an ask and listen mode." Joel then gave the gift of silence.

Starting from the back of the room, there were some chants, "Plant, plant, plant, Joel is a plant."

Everyone enjoyed good-natured ribbing for both Joel and Christa.

She waited until there was silence again. She gestured her hand toward Joel and said, "I would all like you to meet my brother-in-law, Joel."

The group was unsure of whether or not Christa was playing with them or, indeed, if Joel was her brother-in-law.

She waited for the sidebars to stop. Then she said with her broadest smile of the day, "I am just messin' with ya. Joel is not related, he is just very perceptive."

She took three steps to the left so the group could recover their attention and get back to business.

She summarized Joel's on-target comment, "Questions move us from the tell mode to the ask mode." Nodding to Joel, she then continued, "Questions help us engage our audience better, questions help us understand our audience better, and questions make us more empathetic because they help us see things from the viewpoint of others."

She advanced the slide.

Open- and Close-Ended Questions

"Let's develop an arsenal of questioning weapons. We will start with open- and close-ended questions. Let's do a little exercise together. Take five minutes and write down whether you think these are open- or close-ended questions. Then we will discuss them."

She advanced the slide.

> *Identify which kind of question each of these are.*
>
> | | Question | Open / Closed |
> |---|---|---|
> | 1 | Are you familiar with open and closed-ended questions? | |
> | 2 | Which kind of questions do you think are most prevalent? | |
> | 3 | Are you proficient at asking open-ended questions? | |
> | 4 | Do you feel more comfortable asking closed-ended questions? | |
> | 5 | What are the benefits of open-ended questions? | |
> | 6 | Are you sure this is an open-ended question? | |
> | 7 | Is this an easy exercise? | |
> | 8 | How many of these questions do you think you answered correctly? | |
> | 9 | We were all asked questions by our parents; do you think they asked open or closed-ended questions? | |
> | 10 | Will you get the last one right, and if so, will you be happy you are done? | |

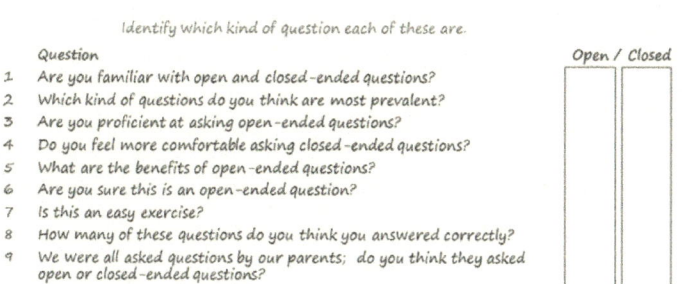

When everyone had completed the exercise, Christa read the questions and reviewed the answers. As she went through the first seven questions, almost everyone in the group got them right.

1. Closed-ended question
2. Open-ended question
3. Closed-ended question
4. Closed-ended question
5. Open-ended question
6. Closed-ended question
7. Closed-ended question

When she read through number eight and gave the answer, a controversy ensued. Many people thought that number eight was a closed-ended question because it had limited answers.

Christa explained, "I love the logic of the limited number of answers. But open- and close-ended questions actually have two dimensions that categorize them. One dimension is the range of answers. The answers to closed-ended questions are binary: yes or no, this or that, etc. There are eleven possible answers to question number eight: zero through ten.

"The other dimension, which helps us identify open- and close-ended questions, is how they start. An open-ended question begins with words like *who, what, where, when,* or *why.* Close-ended questions begin with intransitive verbs or non-action verbs like *are, do, have, will,* etc."

8. Open-ended question

She waited for the explanation to be absorbed and then she finished the exercise.

9. Closed-ended question
10. Closed-ended question

She advanced the slide.

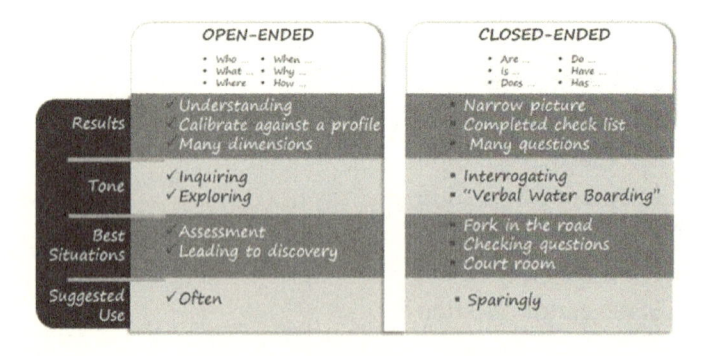

	OPEN-ENDED	CLOSED-ENDED
	• Who • When • What • Why • Where • How	• Are • Do • Is • Have • Does • Has
Results	Understanding Calibrate against a profile Many dimensions	• Narrow picture • Completed check list • Many questions
Tone	✓ Inquiring ✓ Exploring	• Interrogating • "Verbal Water Boarding"
Best Situations	Assessment Leading to discovery	• Fork in the road • Checking questions • Court room
Suggested Use	✓ Often	• Sparingly

"Here is a quick comparison of open-ended and close-ended questions, which might be helpful.

"We looked at the words that begin each type of question. In terms of the results of each type, you can see open-ended questions give us a deeper understanding, and we get more color, whereas close-ended questions give us a narrower picture.

"Let me give you a classic example. A very common question I hear, and my guess you hear as well is, **Would it be helpful if you did . . . blah blah blah.**

"A much better way to ask this is with an open-ended question: **How helpful would it be if you did . . . blah blah blah.** 'Would it be helpful' is likely to produce a yes or no response, whereas 'how helpful' is more likely to draw out some color, indicate degrees of enthusiasm or lack of enthusiasm for the help.

"Open-ended questions are incredibly more efficient. We need to ask fewer questions to get the same information. Perhaps the most important comparison of open- and close-ended questions is the tone.

"The tone of open-ended questions is inquiring and exploring. The tone of close-ended questions is interrogating. One of my clients describes it as verbal waterboarding.

"Open-ended questions work great for most things, and they are especially effective in assessing a situation and executing discovery.

"Closed-ended questions are effective when we are at fork in the road. **Would you like to do this or do that?** We can use closed-ended questions as checking questions. **Did I answer your question?**"

Christa purposely moved to the center of the room. "Based upon what we have discussed so far, which type of question should we use most often, open- or close-ended questions?"

The unanimous response from the group was "open-ended questions."

"Bingo!" She smiled. "But which type of question is used the vast majority of the time?"

They responded, "Closed-ended questions."

"Correct." She extended her hand to the audience, asking for another reply. "Why? Why do we ask closed-ended questions about 70 percent of the time?"

There were different responses, "It is easier." "Not sure." "That's what we learned." "It is less work." "It gives more control."

Christa smiled at the responses offered, and then said, "This is one more thing we can blame on our parents." She paused for a moment, then moved into her parent voice, **"Did you take out the garbage? Did you do your homework? Did you feed the dog? Did you leave the milk out? Did you hit your sister?**

"Modeling is very powerful. It instills both the bad and the good with young minds.

"Another one of my brothers is a lawyer. He is very proficient with questions. He has a three-year-old son named Matt to whom he often asks questions rather than merely telling him what to do. My brother told me last week that Matt used one of my brother's questioning techniques on my brother. My brother often asks Matt at bedtime, **'Son, would you like me to carry you up to bed or would you like to walk up the stairs yourself to bed?'**

"Last week, Matt turned to his dad and, in his three-year-old scratchy voice, said, **'Dad, would you like to play with me sitting on the floor or in your chair?'**

"Modeling is powerful."

She transitioned back to close-ended questions and open-ended questions, "Besides our parents, there seem to be two other reasons we default to close-ended questions when we probably should be asking open-ended questions.

"The first reason, as you already articulated so well, is just it is easier to ask closed-ended questions. Closed-ended questions don't require the same level of brainpower to listen. Closed-ended questions certainly require less brainpower *to develop* the questions.

"The second reason we don't ask open-ended questions is that it requires a questioning strategy to effectively ask open-ended questions. Someone mentioned earlier that closed-ended questions **give us more control**. Actually, they don't, but it sure feels that we have more control. It feels like we are in control because we narrow the range of responses. Narrowing the responses mean we don't have to worry about them taking us off to a flight to never-never land.

"Let's look at this issue of strategy and control differently. Imagine you are visiting two different cities—cities where you do not live. City *A*, you know well—you know all the main streets and highways and how they connect. City *B*, you don't know at all. You are given directions in each city, you have no GPS. In City *A*, which you know well, if you make a wrong turn, what can you do? You can go back to the main street or artery, because you know the city. You are in City *B* with directions, and you make a mistake. What do you have to do? You have to backtrack your steps.

"Most of us approach questions like City *B*. We don't have a strategy, therefore when folks get off-track with a question, we don't know how to get them back to the main streets and highways in the conversation.

"Let me give you another example of having a questioning strategy."

Christa reached back to her little table, which held her laptop. She picked up a deck of cards that was sitting on the table. She held it up to the audience. The deck of cards had a twenty-dollar bill sticking out from the top. She walked over near Jon to whom she threw the marker.

"Jon, I owe you." Pointing to the twenty dollars, she said, "Will you play a game with me?"

He smiled. "For twenty bucks?"

"Yes." Christa handed the deck to someone on the first row and motioned to pass the cards back a few rows to Jon. "So, Jon, here is the deal. If you can guess the top card in that deck, you get to keep the twenty dollars."

He nodded.

"Now, Jon, there are no jokers in the deck, so if you have only one guess, what would be the odds that you will get it right?"

Jon said, "One in fifty-two."

Christa nodded that he was correct. "Not very good odds."

He agreed.

"As I said, I owe you, so I would like to help you guess the correct card and win the twenty dollars. I know what the top card is, but I can't tell you. I can, however, ask you questions so that, perhaps, you can discover the correct card and win the twenty dollars. I would like to work together on this. I would much rather give up the twenty dollars rather than look silly by having you miss the mark." Then she looked directly into his eyes. "Are we good? Are you comfortable with this?"

Jon smiled and said, "Yes."

"Okay, let's get started, Jon. What are the colors of the suits in the deck?"

"Black and red." Jon smiled at the easy question.

"Which do you like best black or red?"

"Red," he answered quickly.

"What are the two red suits?" she continued.

Again, he was quick with his respond. "Hearts and diamonds."

Christa turned to the broader group and said with a smile, "This question is a much trickier question for a woman to answer." Then she turned to Jon, "Which do you like better, hearts or diamonds?"

The group laughed, and most of the room did not hear Jon's answer.

Christa waited until the room was quiet. "Jon, I am not sure that everyone heard your answer to which do you like better, hearts or diamonds?"

Jon repeated his answer, "I said diamonds."

Christa, as a matter of fact, asked, "Which leaves what?"

"Which leave hearts." He sensed what she had done.

Christa held up two fingers about shoulder high, then dipped her hand down low. She offered, "If I tell you that the two of hearts is the lowest heart"—she moved her two fingers above her head—"then what are the top two hearts?"

Jon thought for a moment and said, "The ace and the king of hearts."

"Correct." She didn't hesitate. "Which do you like better between the ace and the king of hearts?"

"The ace," he said with conviction.

Christa repeated his answer to the group, "The ace of hearts." She gave him her now familiar smile. "Jon, might this be a good time to guess?"

Jon got the cue. "It is the ace of hearts."

She signaled him to open the deck and show the room the card. It was the ace of hearts.

"Now, we have a phrase for our teams. Leading someone to the ace of hearts."

Jon tried to pass the twenty dollars forward with the cards.

Christa chided him, "Absolutely not. You keep the money. I keep the cards. That's my policy, and there are no exceptions. Buy someone here a beer."

She turned back to the group. "So how did we get to the ace of hearts?"

The group jumped in, "You led him." "You used questions to get him to the ace of hearts." "There was a questioning strategy."

"Amen. Yes, we got to the ace of hearts because we had a questioning strategy—a questioning strategy, which used almost all open-ended

The Gift of Silence

questions." She paused. "So the question I would have, if I were you, is how do we develop a questioning strategy. Maybe even more specifically, how do we develop a questioning strategy that is easy to use and practical to apply?"

The audience agreed.

Christa advanced the slide. "Here is a questioning strategy on a napkin. It is very simple. We can use it over and over again.

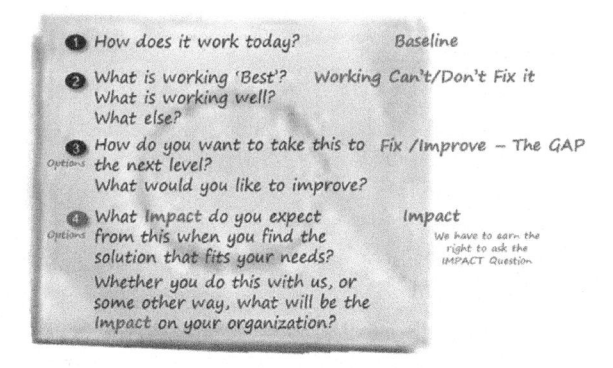

```
1  How does it work today?                    Baseline

2  What is working 'Best'?      Working Can't/Don't Fix it
   What is working well?
   What else?

3  How do you want to take this to    Fix/Improve – The GAP
Options  the next level?
   What would you like to improve?

4  What Impact do you expect          Impact
Options  from this when you find the         We have to earn the
   solution that fits your needs?            right to ask the
                                             IMPACT Question
   Whether you do this with us, or
   some other way, what will be the
   Impact on your organization?
```

"Let's look at the first question. This gives us a baseline of where we are. We might ask, '**How do you do XYZ today?**' or '**How does it work today?**' or '**How do you do that now?**'

"Once we have a baseline, then we can ask the next question. Think for a moment. How does this typically work in conversations? When folks get a baseline of how things are working today, what are the two things they almost always do next?"

The group responded, "Pitch their message." "Explain how they can fix what they are doing today." "Ask a question about what they don't like in terms of how things are working."

"Well said." She continued, "You are absolutely right. After we find out how things work, we naturally take one of two paths:

> We either *pitch* how we can help them do things differently, or

> we pose questions to find out *what we can fix* for them—we ask them questions about how they might want to improve what they are doing.

"These are exactly the wrong things to do. If we pitch . . . into what kind of soil are we casting our messages?"

The group answered, "Cement or the rocky soil, certainly not the rich soil."

"Bingo. What is wrong with the second natural path of asking questions, finding out what we could fix?" She stopped and waited for the group to ruminate on the question. There were no volunteers. She walked to her laptop and prepared to advance her slide. "This is a critical communication principle, particularly germane to sales and marketing." She advanced the slide.

You Can Never ... Tell People Their Children Are Ugly.

The participants laughed at the picture.

"The way we do things today as organizations are our children. They have parents and other relatives who hold these processes, procedures, and solutions dear. If we jump in trying to fix things prematurely, then we run a horrific risk of **'telling people their children are ugly.'"**

She looked around the room to calibrate how well this idea resonated with them. Feeling comfortable that they understood the importance of the 'ugly children' principle, she posed another question, "So how do we avoid telling people that their children are ugly?"

Initially, there were no responses. After a few moments, a man in the second row left asked, "Could you go back to the napkin?"

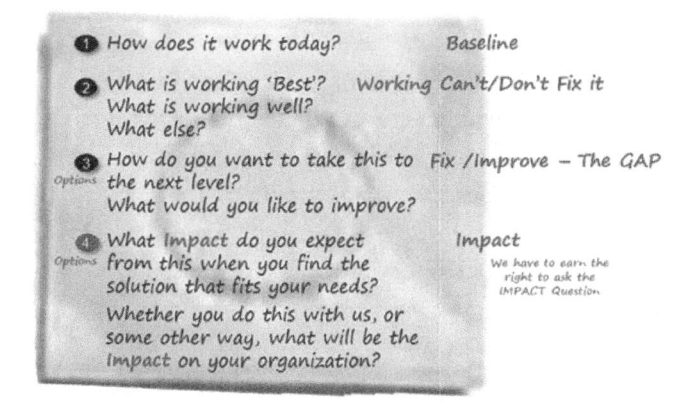

> ❶ How does it work today? Baseline
>
> ❷ What is working 'Best'? Working Can't/Don't Fix it
> What is working well?
> What else?
>
> ❸ How do you want to take this to Fix /Improve — The GAP
> Options the next level?
> What would you like to improve?
>
> ❹ What Impact do you expect Impact
> Options from this when you find the We have to earn the
> solution that fits your needs? right to ask the
> IMPACT Question
> Whether you do this with us, or
> some other way, what will be the
> Impact on your organization?

She gladly backtracked the slide, which showed the napkin strategy for a second time. "What are the questions in the second step of napkin strategy questions? Yes, what is working best? *What is working well? What else is working well?* Why would we ask these questions after we get a baseline?"

"So we can find out what they like about what they are doing." "To avoid offending them." "So we don't tell them their children are ugly." The group shared the enthusiasm.

"Perfect! Beautifully said. Most of the time, when we ask what is the 'working best,' they naturally do what?"

A voice shouted, "They naturally start to tell us what is not working."

"Bingo. At least 60 percent of the time the 'best question' naturally morphs into a discussion about what needs to be improved. This provides us rich soil for our messaging."

The group spent several minutes sharing examples, where they wished they had used this questioning strategy on a napkin and a few situations where they had instinctively focused on what was working well, and it paid dividends.

Christa transitioned back to the napkin snapshot. "Earlier we discussed the why and impact statements. You can see how the fourth question in the napkin strategy opens up the why by engaging in an impact discussion. Although the impact question is a key part of the napkin strategy, we always have to earn the right to ask the impact question. We might not execute all four parts in one interview or one meeting or one session." She surveyed the room.

"Any questions on the napkin strategy question or questioning strategies in general?"

A woman near the top on the left raised her hand and said, "I loved the card game as a metaphor, but can you really lead people to the ace of hearts in real life?"

Christa nodded. "Thank you for the question. The simple answer is yes, but it does take skill. I will give you an example.

"As an aside, one of the reasons I am such a passionate believer in the power of questions is the impact questions have on healthy dialogues at home, particularly between parents and kids. There is, however, a downside. As I mentioned before, kids learn from modeling, and so they can use what they learn against us. My son did this with my husband.

"A few years ago, my husband decided to buy himself a cool convertible that he couldn't drive in the winter. So to solve the problem, he bought an old jeep. My oldest son was fourteen at the time, so the plan was to give my son the car when he turned sixteen, which would make all our lives easier . . . if not a little scarier. About two months before our son's sixteenth birthday, my husband was driving the jeep with my son, and my son asked his dad, 'Hey, Dad, do you notice anything weird about the steering wheel?' My husband looked at the steering wheel and said, 'No.' My son, then, asked, 'Hey, Dad, where is the airbag?'

"At that point, my husband came to the devastating realization that he had bought the last year jeep you could buy that didn't have an airbag. My son let the problem marinate a little, and then threw my husband the grenade, 'Hey, Dad, how are you going to feel about your sixteen-year-old driving a car without an airbag?' My husband knew exactly where my son was going with this and said, 'I'm going to feel just fine.' So my son said, 'How is Mom going to feel about it?'"

The audience groaned.

Christa gave two thumbs-up. "The boy played the 'Mom' card. Love it. As a result of my son's great questioning, he got a car that was three years newer, because we immediately traded in the one without the airbag for one that did have an airbag."

Christa turned to the woman who asked the question, "That is leading someone to the ace of hearts. Did I answer your question?"

The woman nodded.

"Let's take a ten-minute break, and then continue our discussion of questions."

As soon as she called the break, Christa quickly strode to the restroom. When she returned, she still had three minutes before they were to resume. She checked her phone. She responded to her brother's earlier text about her Dad, *Spoke to him two days ago. Sent him a couple of texts this morning, but no answers as yet. Is everything okay?*

She waited for a reply from her brother, who was also in Los Angeles. No reply came, and it was time to start the workshop again. She turned off her phone.

Ten minutes later, her brother called and left her a voicemail. "Christa, I know you probably have your phone off. Please call me. Dad didn't show up at the office yesterday, and no one has heard from him—not very Dad-like. Please call me as soon as you get this."

Chapter 12

After the break, she thanked them for their prompt return and said, "Let's discuss two other types of questions that we can put in our arsenal: spectrum questions and strategic questions.

"First, spectrum questions: What are spectrum questions and when might we use this questioning weapon?

"Spectrum questions are a specific type of open-ended question that creates a spectrum for folks to put themselves on, and in doing so, provides no value judgment.

"Spectrum questions are perfect for situations where asking the question is problematic. Picture it as a situation where you are sticking your head in the lion's mouth or you are trying to pull the sword from the stone.

"Let's say that your organization has just announced that you are moving your office across the city. One of your key folks lives right near your current office, so you know this could potentially have a job-changing impact for them. You need an open and honest picture of where they are. You might pose a spectrum question like,

We all just got some news. For some folks, this is no big

deal, for others, it is devastating, and there are probably a whole bunch in the middle? Where are you?

"The question is open-ended and has no value judgment. We provided a spectrum on which they can place themselves anywhere on that spectrum. Therefore, we are likely to get an honest answer and avoid offending them with the question.

"Let's try another one. The situation is that we have proposed an idea or solution, which seems to have gotten a pretty good response. We don't know how serious they are about wanting to move ahead or not. We might ask,

At this point in the discussion, some teams have a clear idea of when they want to be live with a solution like this and some teams are not clear. Gift of silence, or **where are you?"**

The group posed a couple of questions.

"Let me give you one more example, and then I will give you a chance to create your own spectrum questions.

"A few years ago, I went to China for a couple weeks on business. We had several PCs in the house, because my oldest son was very technical and liked to build PCs from scratch. We also had rules—even a contract—about appropriate websites, etc. So when I got home, I did what most parents would do. I checked the history files. Wow! At first, I was embarrassed, and then I was furious. My son violated my trust and our agreement. I couldn't wait for him to get home from school so I could rip into him.

"Luckily, before he got home, I calmed myself and stepped back. He was a great kid and had never done anything like this. I realized that I needed to handle this appropriately, and I needed to find out what was really going on. I said to myself, 'I need to walk the talk here.' So I prepared for our conversation the same way I would prepare for an important conversation with a client. I even prepared a spectrum question.

"I sat down with him, and I said, 'Son, I need to discuss something serious with you. I went through the history files on the computers, and wow—way out of bounds. So there is either something I don't understand about what happened or there has been a major violation of our agreement.'

"He said to me, 'Mom, can I ask you a question?' There was a pause. 'Did we have any visitors while you were gone?'

"Then it hit me like a brick. My brother from California had come to visit while I was gone. He had driven my car, and there were matches in the car from strip clubs—so I knew who the culprit was. By the way, I had a different conversation with my brother.

The group chimed in, "I bet." "That must have been interesting."

"If I had just asked my son a clumsy question, I could have damaged years of trust and respect. The spectrum saved me." She made a writing motion in the air. "Okay, I would like you all to try creating a spectrum question. Think about a tricky situation—one where you are sticking your head in the lion's mouth or trying to get the sword out of the stone. Create a spectrum of possible responses you could get. Make sure there is no value judgment so someone could safely place themselves on that spectrum. Then turn it into a spectrum question."

The group wrote down their questions. Seven participants shared their questions, and the group discussed them.

Strategic Questions

"Let's look at one more type of question for your questioning arsenal. The strategic question.

"So what is a strategic question?

"It is a very high-level open-ended question that is simply and strategically posed to create a waterfall of information.

"What does that mean?

"Let's first look at a typical way we would ask probing questions. We will start with a fun example: homework. Everyone here at some point in their academic career has been asked about their homework. Some of you are parents going through this yourself now, where you are regularly asking about your child's homework.

"This is typically done in what we might call a 'poke' and 'listen' approach. It goes something like this:

Did you do your homework?

How much do you have to do?

How much time will that take?

"If we don't get the answers we wanted, we might even resort to . . .

Don't you care about your grades?

"Or the ill-fated question to our seven-year-old, **'Don't you want to go to a good college?'**

"Notice that the poke and listen is a combination of open-ended and closed-ended questions poking in several areas: the state of their homework, the possible gap between completed and not completed homework, the student's commitment to good grades, and the student's grasp of the impact of their grades on their future.

"So how might we do this with a strategic question? We might simply ask, 'Let's talk homework.' Then we give the gift of silence.

"The first thing out of the student's mouth will tell us the world. If we ask, 'Let's talk homework,' and they respond, **'Got it done. I was going to ask for help with the math, but I figured it out. The English homework was a pain, but the Biology stuff was fun,'** what does that tell us?"

"They are on top of it." "Good-to-go." "We probably don't need to probe much more," the group offered.

Christa painted the contrast. "What if we ask, 'Let's talk homework,' and the student responds 'Why do we get so much homework. It is a waste of time. Why are you always asking me about homework?'

"The homework isn't done." "Good thing you asked." "Something is rotten in Denmark," the group responded.

"Bingo. Well done. You can see that a good strategic question is very simple, yet it sets up a situation where the first thing out of their mouth is going to tell us the world. Once we get that first snapshot of what is top of mind for them, then we can listen for the other areas that are important to us. They might be freely divulged, or we might have to probe. Perhaps, they never mention English, which has been a proverbial thorn in their side. We might ask, **What was the English like?"**

Christa took some questions, and they wrote down some strategic questions and discussed them as a group.

"Our purpose for this section was to give you an arsenal of questioning tools. We looked at open-ended and closed-ended questions, a questioning strategy on a napkin, spectrum questions, and strategic questions. What questions do you have on questions?"

There were a couple of questions that the group answered together.

Christa turned to the group and asked, "What question should be our go-to question, the question we probably ask the most?"

There were a few guesses.

She smiled and said, "Tell me more. Tell me more should be the question we ask the most." She waited. "May I have your permission to put a gender slant on this?"

The group seemed a bit confused.

Christa smiled even wider. "Guys have a much harder time asking the question 'tell me more.' If you don't believe me, try practicing at home."

There was a fairly raucous agreement on both sides of the gender divide that this was true.

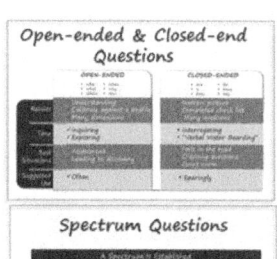

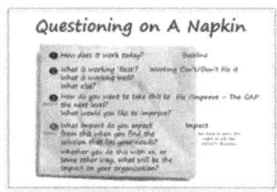

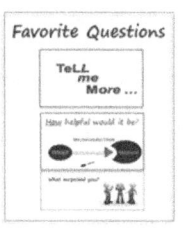

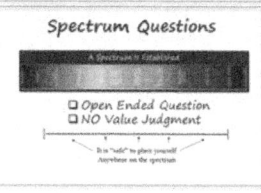

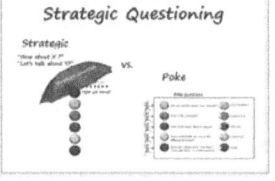

Chapter 13

Listening

"You have been amazing today, thank you. We are going to cover one more topic. We are going to end with listening. I am always conflicted about whether we should start with this topic or end with this topic. But either way, it is fitting that if our objective is to be better communicators, then we need to be better listeners.

"There is a great deal of sage advice out there regarding listening. I want to take a quick look at eight different points of advice, and then I am going to give you a simple self-assessment tool so that you can chart your own path to improved listening."

She advanced the slide.

"Here are eight things we might consider before we do our self-assessment.

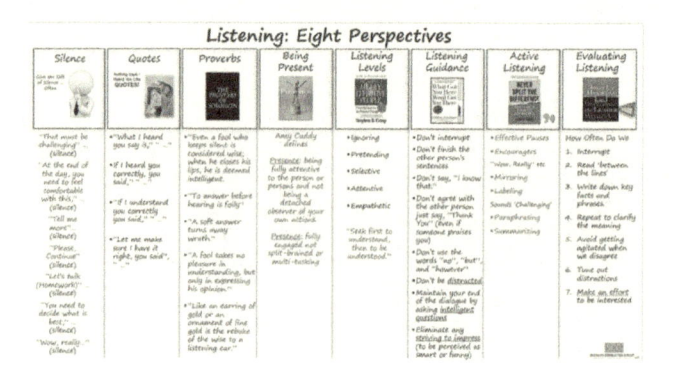

"First, the topic, which kicked off our day, was the gift of silence. The gift of silence is key for all of us to be more accomplished listeners.

"Second, the power of quotes is critical to deep listening. Nothing says 'I heard you like a quote.'

"There are also excellent written sources to help better understand listening. I have listed six excellent books that provide some great insights on listening:

The book of Proverbs by Solomon

Presence by Amy Cuddy

The Seven Habits of Highly Effective People by Stephen Covey

What Got You Here Won't Get You There by Marshall Goldsmith

Never Split the Difference by Chris Voss

The Gift of Silence

Developing the Leader within You by John Maxwell

"Let's take a snapshot on listening from each of these excellent sources.

"The book of Proverbs by Solomon has many sage words about listening. Two of my favorites are

> **A fool takes no pleasure in understanding, but only in expressing his opinion.**
>
> **Even a fool who keeps silent is considered wise; when he closes his lips, he is deemed intelligent."**

"If you haven't read Amy Cuddy's book, *Presence*, do so. There is great wisdom in there, not the least of which is her definition of being present: *'Presence*: **being fully attentive to the person or persons and not being a detached observer of your own actions.'** Being fully attentive to the person is critical to good listening.

"In Stephen Covey's classic, he provides two powerful perspectives on listening. First, '**seek first to** understand then to be understood.' He also provides a very insightful perspective on levels of listening:

Ignoring
Pretending
Selective
Attentive
Empathetic

"Marshall Goldsmith in *What Got You Here Won't Get You There* provides some terrific guidance and guardrails for listening:

Don't interrupt.

Don't finish the other person's sentences.

Don't say, 'I know that.'

Don't agree with the other person, just say, 'thank you' (even if someone praises you).

Don't use the words 'no,' 'but,' and 'however.'

Don't be *distracted*.

Maintain your end of the dialogue by asking *intelligent questions*.

Eliminate any *striving to impress* [to be perceived as smart or funny].

"In *Never Split the Difference*, Chris Voss puts some teeth on good listening and gives some definition to active listening:

Effective pauses

Encouragers—'Wow, really,' etc.

Mirroring

Paraphrasing

Summarizing

"John Maxwell provides some challenging self-assessment insights in *Developing the Leader within You*. He asks us to look at how often we do the following:

Interrupt

Read between the lines

Write down key facts and phrases

Repeat to clarify the meaning

Avoid getting agitated when we disagree

Tune out distractions

Make an effort to be interested

"Listening is a tremendous challenge for all of us, and if we are honest with ourselves, we would probably all agree that there is plenty of room for each of us to improve. With that in mind, I would like each to take about ten minutes to do this listening self-assessment. Let me describe what is here, and then we can discuss how to use it."

She had the last person in each row pass a copy of the listening assessment sheet down the row, so everyone in the room had it in front of them. She also showed it on the screen.

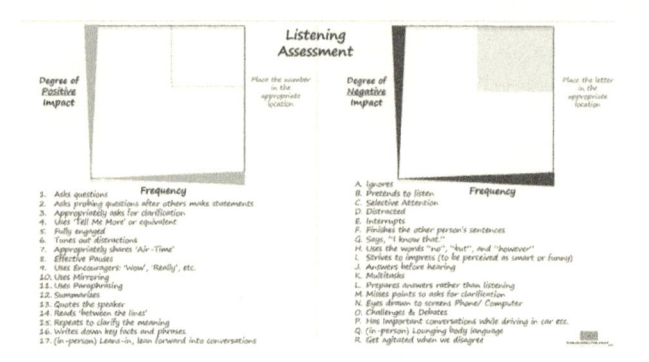

Listening Assessment

Left (green box): Degree of Positive Impact (vertical) vs. Frequency (horizontal). Place the number in the appropriate location.

1. Asks questions
2. Asks probing questions after others make statements
3. Appropriately asks for clarification
4. Uses 'Tell Me More' or equivalent
5. Fully engaged
6. Tunes out distractions
7. Appropriately shares 'Air-Time'
8. Effective Pauses
9. Uses Encouragers: 'Wow', 'Really', etc.
10. Uses Mirroring
11. Uses Paraphrasing
12. Summarizes
13. Quotes the speaker
14. Reads 'between the lines'
15. Repeats to clarify the meaning
16. Writes down key facts and phrases
17. (In-person) Leans-in, lean forward into conversations

Right (red box): Degree of Negative Impact (vertical) vs. Frequency (horizontal). Place the letter in the appropriate location.

A. Ignores
B. Pretends to listen
C. Selective Attention
D. Distracted
E. Interrupts
F. Finishes the other person's sentences
G. Says, "I know that."
H. Uses the words "no", "but", and "however"
I. Strives to impress (to be perceived as smart or funny)
J. Answers before hearing
K. Multitasks
L. Prepares answers rather than listening
M. Misses points so asks for clarification
N. Eyes down to screens Phone/Computer
O. Challenges & Debates
P. Has important conversations while driving in car etc.
Q. (In-person) Lounging body language
R. Gets agitated when we disagree

"On the left-hand side, you can see that in the green box the horizontal line is *frequency*—how often we do something. The vertical axis is the *degree of positive impact*—our view of the positive impact this behavior typically has.

"On the right-hand side in the red box, the horizontal line is frequency—how often we do something. The vertical axis is the *degree of negative impact*—our view of the negative impact this behavior typically has.

"Below both the green box and the red box is a set of behaviors listed. The green box has numbers next to the behaviors, and the red box has letters next to the behaviors.

"For both boxes, place the numbers and the letters where they belong based on your assessment of your typical behaviors [the numbers for green, and the letters for red]. As an example, number one, **'asks questions.'** If you do that all the time, put the number one to the far right in the green box. If you think it has a very high impact in terms of good listening, then put the number one high and to the right.

"Another example might be in the red box. Let's take number two: **'Pretends to listen.'** Perhaps it is something we do some of the time, but when we do it, we can sense that it has a terrible impact on the conversation. So we might put a number high in the box, but in the middle in terms of frequency.

"The result of doing this is that you will end up with a scattergram in the green box and a scattergram in the red box.

"Do the green box—positive behaviors first. Then do the red box—the negative behaviors next. Take about ten minutes."

The green strengths box had the following:

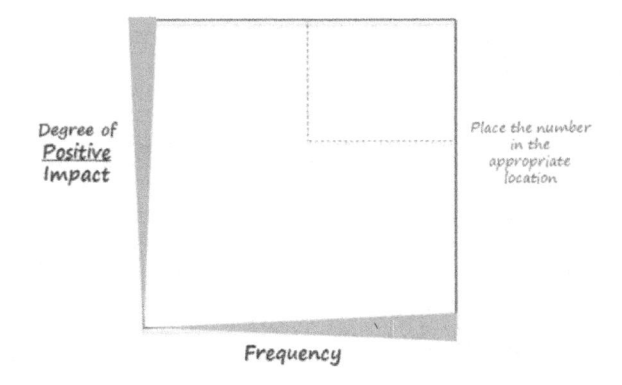

Degree of Positive Impact

Place the number in the appropriate location

Frequency

1. Asks questions
2. Asks probing questions after others make statements
3. Appropriately asks for clarification
4. Uses "tell me more" or equivalent
5. Fully engaged
6. Tunes out distractions
7. Appropriately shares air time
8. Effective pauses
9. Uses encouragers: "Wow," "really," etc.
10. Uses mirroring
11. Uses paraphrasing
12. Summarizes

13. Quotes the speaker
14. Reads between the lines
15. Repeats to clarify the meaning
16. Writes down key facts and phrases
(In-person) Leans in, lean forward into conversations

The red improve box had the following:

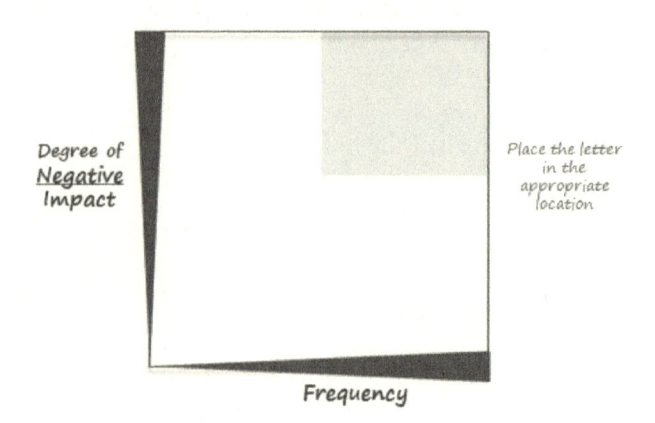

Degree of Negative Impact (y-axis) vs *Frequency* (x-axis) — Place the letter in the appropriate location

A. Ignores
B. Pretends to listen
C. Selective attention
D. Distracted
E. Interrupts
F. Finishes the other person's sentences
G. Says, "I know that."
H. Uses the words no, but, and however
I. Strives to impress (to be perceived as smart or funny)
J. Answers before hearing
K. Multitasks
L. Prepares answers rather than listening
M. Misses points, so asks for clarification
N. Eyes are drawn to screens of phones/computers
O. Challenges and debates

    P. *Has important conversations while driving in the car, etc.*
    Q. *(In-person) Lounging body language*
    R. *Get agitated when we disagree*

The group worked on the exercise for ten minutes.

Christa reconvened, "Looks like everyone completed the exercise. So your thoughts?" She purposely posed a strategic question.

The group responded with a barrage of comments: "I suck; this was hard." "I thought I was a good listener." "The multitasking thing really spoke to me." "There is a lot to being a good listener." "What did you say?"

There were some laughs at the attempt of irony.

Christa redirected, "This exercise is not meant to make us feel bad. But it does remind me every time I read through it how high the bar is for good listening and how often I miss the mark."

There were many affirmative head nods.

"So how shall we then live? How can we take the insights we get from an exercise like this and drive change in our behaviors, which improve our listening?" She took a step to the left. "Let's start on the green side. The positive behaviors. There is a great deal of research to show that top performers in every field know how to leverage their strengths. My guess is we have many card-carrying perfectionists in this group. The tendency for most is to jump to red—things to improve. However, the best thing we can do is leverage our strengths." She stepped back to the right.

"Let's be specific in terms of leveraging our strengths. I want you to take a couple minutes and look at the listening things you do well. Ask yourself, 'Which two things, which I do pretty well, should I leverage more often? Which strengths can I maximize?' Write them down."

Christa moved across the front of the room, observing the participants as they made their choices. After almost five minutes, she drew their focus to the negative behaviors. "Okay, now let's look at the negative behaviors in the red box. Pick one you know you need to work on because of either impact or frequency or both."

Again, she paced the front of the room and waited for everyone to write down the behaviors they wanted to improve.

She captured their attention. "Okay, so now you have a very simple plan to improve your listening: two strengths to leverage and one area to improve. Professionals practice. This is where discipline and self-respect kick in. This little listening plan can either be a dusty note in our notebook or a platform to take our listening skills to another level."

Chapter 14

Summary

Christa showed on the screen the image with which she started the day:

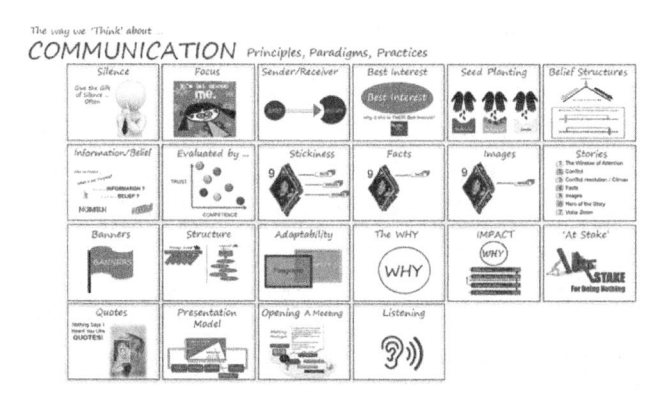

She gave her broadest smile of the day. "I want to thank you all for being so engaged today. For asking some great questions. For challenging things that were uncomfortable or unclear. For bringing your sense of humor to our discussion today. You have made this a great day for me. I hope this was a productive and enjoyable day for you." She gave the gift of silence.

"I told you when we started, it would be a full day and that you would probably need your track shoes. We have covered many topics related to improving our communications. Just a little while ago, we discussed questions." She flipped back to the questions summary slide. "We did some work on open-ended and closed-ended questions, introduced a questioning strategy on a napkin, looked at the use of spectrum questions for questioning in delicate areas, played with strategic questions, and discussed the imperative of 'tell me more.'"

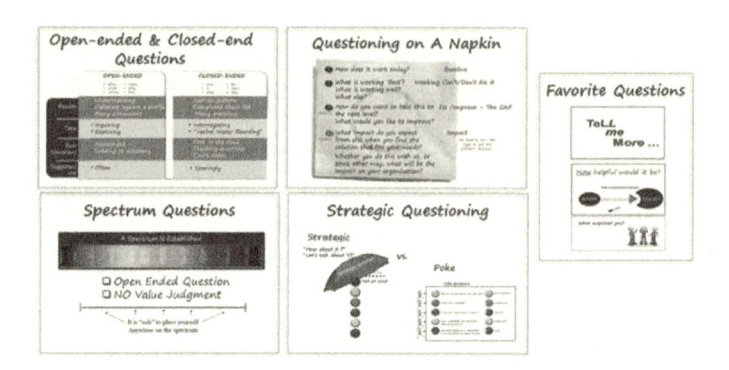

She flipped back to the communication summary slide.

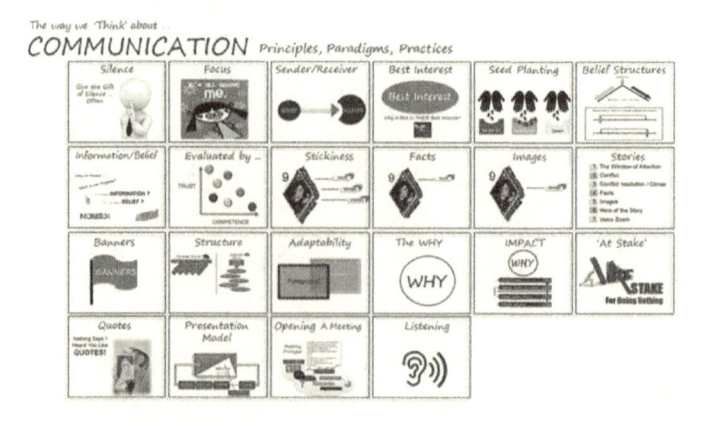

"Before we discussed questions, we went through a bevy of communication topics:

> We have discussed the gift of silence, making our communications about *them* and not *us*.

We discussed the best interest principle and how we get evaluated by others in terms of trust and competence.

We talked about planting messages in the rich soil and the rocky soil.

We looked at the importance of belief structures and calibrating the belief structure. We had a conversation about focusing on belief versus information when we present.

We took a little walk into the brain and peeked at how it processes information. We discussed into some detail the nine weeping widows, or the use of facts, images, and stories.

We even looked at a seven-step structure for creating very short thirty-second stories.

We defined banners and how they are used.

We put questions of structure on the table and examined the dump truck versus the layered structure to presenting.

We challenged ourselves to be more adaptable by anticipating that our presentations will be shortened, and we landed on the importance of identifying the foreground and background material as the key to this adaptability.

We had a messaging physics discussion and recognized that the pull of gravity on most messaging is the how. We contrasted this natural pull of gravity to the vehicle for impetus to action—focus on the why.

We gave substance to the why by describing how we can ascend the mountain of the why through impact statements. We got into some detail about the power of level three and level four impact statements. We had some lively conversation about how these emotional impacts and the dollars and cents impact statements are used together to provide unparalleled impetus to action.

We continued our messaging physics discussion with a look at Newton's first law—the law of inertia. We identified a specific way to overcome the challenge of a body at rest will remain at rest. We gave this villain the name Dr. Do Nothing. We agreed that our best weapon against Dr. Do Nothing is identifying what is at stake if we do nothing.

We discussed the power of quotes and how quotes say, 'I heard you.'

We turned a critical eye to the way folks normally present, and then we looked at a very different presentation model—a model that starts about *them*, morphs to *us*, and ends with *them*.

We drilled down on the presentation model and looked at how we open the meeting with questions: the meeting prologue, how we provide a snapshot of their environment, how we articulate the audience's objectives, how we do our normal stuff in the middle, and how we close with a summary of their objectives—and perhaps, if we have the courage, a question about how we did in terms of helping them with their objectives.

We briefly looked at several resources that had good advice for us on listening, and then took a little self-assessment exercise on listening. We identified two areas of strengths and one area for improvement.

As a matter of fact, one of the questions we addressed this morning when we started was how to get the most out of this workshop. What was my counsel to you?"

Jon, who did the marker exchange, answered, "You said to pick two things that we discussed that we do, and two things discussed that we probably should do. Leverage the good stuff and change the other stuff. Then put the other material aside for another day."

The room erupted with applause.

Christa smiled. She was tempted to reach for a marker, but resisted. "Thank you. Well said. So let's do that. Excluding the things you already wrote down for the listening exercise, write down two areas where you had an epiphany about your strengths that you want to leverage more often. Take a few minutes to do that."

It took about five minutes for everyone to record two strengths to leverage.

"Okay, now let's pick two areas to improve or two new approaches, which you feel would really help your communications."

This took about ten minutes for everyone to write down their thoughts.

"Super. Thank you for taking the exercise seriously." She gave her widest smile of the day. "When we started this morning, we discussed the shared objective of leaving this room at the end of the day equipped with an arsenal of approaches to make us better communicators." She paused. "How did we do?"

The room broke into applause.

Christa bowed her head in gratitude. "Thank you for the great privilege and the fun of working together today. Send me notes and call me and let me know how else I can help. Thank you."

The participants stood and began packing their things. It was 3:57 p.m.

As was often the case, the participants formed an informal receiving line to say goodbye to Christa, thank her, or ask her questions.

At four twenty, she had spoken to everyone in the line, so she pulled her phone from her pocket.

She continued to pack her things as she listened to her brother's first voicemail followed by a second voicemail. "Christa, you really need to call me."

She dialed her brother. He answered, "Hey. Sorry to leave your voicemails like that." He paused.

She spoke, "What is going on?"

"Christa, we are not sure, but Dad was not at work yesterday, he has not been to work today, and no one has heard from him. You know how responsible he is. Bob Karmann is on his way over to Dad's place. Bob was at the office, he is forty-five minutes closer than I am to Dad's place. He is going to check on him."

The Gift of Silence

The both of them stood in silence, fighting off the bad dreams of what might be.

Her brother spoke first, "Please keep your phone on. I will call you as soon as I hear from Bob."

Christa finished packing up her laptop and pulled her rolling bag from the luggage alcove. She made a quick stop at the restroom. Her ride to Logan airport at this time of day was likely to be between one to two hours; she took a 'comfort break' in anticipation of the traffic.

As she walked from the restroom to the lobby, her phone vibrated in her pocket. It was her brother. He hesitated; he struggled to push the words out, "He is gone."

"What do you mean, is he missing? Is he . . ." She couldn't say it.

"Looks like he had a heart attack. Bob found him in his chair. He's gone."

They both cried. There was nothing to say. There were no words. There was no comprehension. Nothing was going to change the horror of the moment.

Every breath Christa took felt like it was made from the bottom of a dark lake. The silence hung on the drip of each tear.

They both finally spoke almost at the same time, "I love you." It was the only thing they could say.

Christa added, "I wish I were there. I will get a flight out as soon as I can."

"Call me later when you get your flights. I'm going to go over to Dad's place." Then her brother hung up the phone.

They disconnected and began processing the nightmare on their own.

Christa walked through the lobby to meet her ride to the airport. She would have plenty of time in the car to change her flight and get a flight to Los Angeles.

While she was walking through the lobby, Viola, one of the women from the workshop, saw Christa walking to the door sobbing. She walked up to Christa. "You are obviously upset, honey, what is the matter?"

Christa didn't lift her head but spoke to her shoes in almost a whisper, "I just found out my dad died."

Viola threw her large, engulfing arms around Christa. She just held her in silence for a couple minutes. "My mom used to say that there are times when we need to just speak with our arms." Viola continued to embrace Christa and held her while waves of reality, loss, and confusion continued to pound Christa.

Neither could tell how long they embraced while Christa struggled through the waves.

Finally, both could sense that Christa had regained her emotional equilibrium.

It was time to go and get in the car.

As Viola let go, she said, "You will be in my prayers."

Christa nodded and struggled to get the words out, "Thank you. I will definitely need them."

The car Christa had ordered pulled up to the curb a few steps outside the lobby door.

Viola said goodbye, and Christa said, "Thank you."

As the driver was loading her bag into the trunk and Christa slid into the back seat, it struck her that a new chapter had begun. She was now the oldest in the family. She was not ready for that, she was not ready to lose her dad—we never are. A new chapter awaited her—ready or not.

Summary of Communication Topics

Topic	Explanation
Gift of Silence	*The power of silence after a question or statement*
Focus	*Making the focus of the discussion about them and not ourselves*
Belief Structures	*The power of calibrating belief structures*
Best Interest	*The imperative of first understanding why something is in their best interest*
Rich Soil, Rocky Soil	*The importance of planting our messaging seeds in their specific words and ideas*
Stickiness	*How the brain determines what is sticky or not*
Facts	*The use of sticky facts*
Images	*The use of image words vs. concept words*
Stories	*Building thirty-second stories*
Information/Belief	*The always on objective of belief*
Evaluated By	*A framework for how people intuitively evaluate the likelihood that they will buy what we are saying or selling*
Banners	*An image-based approach to messages*
Structure	*Dump truck vs. layered approach to messaging*
Adaptability	*The role of foreground and background in adaptability*

Why	*Driving to the why vs. the how*
Impact Statements	*Four levels of impact statements*
At Stake	*Breaking sedentary inertia by focusing on what is at stake*
Quotes	*The use of quotes in dialogue and writing*
Presentation Model	*A simple customer model for presenting*
Listening	*A self-assessment tool for listening skills*

QUESTIONS

Topic	Explanation
Open and Closed-Ended Questions	The effective and appropriate use of open-ended and closed-ended questions
Questioning on a Napkin	A simple strategy for probing
Spectrum Questions	An approach to asking questions in situations where the topic is delicate, and the purpose is to uncover existing beliefs
Strategic Questions	An approach to asking simple questions, which reveal what is top of mind and uncovers a great deal of information without incessant probing

INDEX

A

adaptability, 86, 161
agendas, 21–22
airbag, 131
air time, 18
Ann (client), 20
answers
    five-second, 78
    low-level, 93
approaches
    cement, 33
    first messaging, 66
    poke and listen, 136
    readiness, 29–31
    rich soil, 34–36, 128, 130, 153, 161
    rocky soil, 34–35, 128, 153, 161
association/connection, 57
attributes, 41, 59, 63
axes, 111, 146

B

Babson Executive Conference Center, 9, 16, 70
background, 87, 108, 110, 153
banners, 71–74, 161
behaviors
    negative, 147, 150
    positive, 147, 149
beliefs, 44
boy, fourteen-year-old, 58
brain, 56–57
brainwork misconceptions, 38
brother, 122
buy-in, 47
buy pie, 50

C

calibration, 29, 39–40, 73
cards, 123–24, 126
CEO, 65–66, 79
Christa (speaker), 4, 26, 101, 118, 157–59
climax, 64
commercials, 63–64
communications, 11, 13, 15, 22, 41, 44, 52, 65, 99, 151
    all about me, 17, 21–22, 25, 44, 117
communication topics, 11, 25, 52, 152–53, 161
communicators, effective, 22, 63, 90–91
competence, 50–52, 153
complexity, 74
conflict, 64
Covey, Stephen, 143

Seven Habits of Highly Effective People, The, 143
cropping, 21
Cuddy, Amy, 143
    Presence, 143

D

Dad (Christa's father), 1, 28, 53, 156–57
deck
    of cards, 123
    standard presentation, 104, 106
Developing the Leader within You (Maxwell), 145
dialogue, 104, 106
dimensions, 119
discipline, 29, 31, 36, 78, 80–81, 150
discussion
    at stake, 96–97, 162
    why and how, 90, 92
Draper, Don, 48
dream, ambitious, 1

E

emotions, 57–58
empathy, 19, 32
environment section, 112–13
Eric (participant), 76
evaluation, 46, 161

F

facts, 59, 161
flight, 123, 157–58
focus, 17, 161
foreground, 86–87, 153
frequency, 146

G

Goldsmith, Marshall, 143
    What Got You Here Won't Get You There, 143

grammar
    first person, 68
    second person, 68
    third person, 68–69
group habit, 74

H

Harrison (participant), 79
hippocampus, 57–58
Hoffman, Dustin, 56
homework, 137
Howie (participant), 48
Hudson, Tom, 40
husband (Christa's), 131

I

imagery, 62
impacts, 92
    emotional, 58, 95
    negative, 146
    positive, 95
impact scale, 93
impact statements, 93–97, 162
implementation, great, 4–5
inertia, law of, 96
information, 38, 44–45
In Never Split the Difference (Voss), 144
intent, 50, 114
interruption, 21

J

Joel (participant), 101–2, 118
Jon (participant), 26, 74
Joy (participant), 102

K

Karmann, Bob, 156
kids, 131
King, Martin Luther, Jr., 61

L

layering, 82
lecture hall, 7
listening, 141, 145, 162
    active, 144
    book sources, 142
    guidance and guardrails for, 143
    improvement plan for, 150
    levels of, 143
    self-assessment insights of, 145, 149
Lou (Christa's boss), 45–46
Luke (participant), 115
lunch, 9

M

Madison (participant), 78
Madison Avenue, 64
Marc (Christa's friend), 1–3
Mari (participant), 44
Marissa (participant), 9, 81
Mark (Christa's teammate), 45–46
marker, 25, 27–28, 69
Matt (son of Christa's brother), 122
Maurice (participant), 102
Maxwell, John, 145
    Developing the Leader within You, 145
meeting prologue, 113, 115
meetings, in-person, 45
message assessment, 74
messages, 11, 19, 23, 27–36, 40–42, 55–56, 58, 66, 69, 72–73, 82, 86–87, 89, 91, 115–17
messaging, 19
    sales, 91
messaging physics, 91, 96, 153–54
modes, 17, 19, 66, 75, 117–18
monologue, 104, 106
Myers Briggs, 20

N

nine weeping widows, 59, 69
notetaking, 103

O

objectives, 9, 115–16
OneNote, 103

P

Paul (participant), 100
perceived success, 18, 22
Phil (participant), 74, 104
presence, 143
Presence (Cuddy), 143
presentations, 41, 43, 45, 75, 77, 83–87, 99–100, 106–7, 109
    external, 109, 111
    internal, 107, 113
    standard, 111
principles
    seed planting, 32–33
    ugly children, 129
priorities, 21
    white board of, 95
problem, 100
    group layering, 80
pronouns, 20
Proverbs, 62, 141–43

Q

questions, 19, 117–18, 154, 163
    closed-ended, 19, 119, 121, 123
    close-ended, 120
    impact, 92
    open-ended, 120–21, 123
    spectrum, 133, 135, 163
    strategic, 136, 163
quotes, 99, 101–2, 104, 115, 154, 162

R

Rain Man, 56
receiver, 28
return on investments (ROI), 94–95

S

sales team, 34
savant disease, 56
selling, 46
sender, 28
Seth (self-espoused talker), 16
*Seven Habits of Highly Effective People,
    The* (Covey), 142
Solomon, 142
son (Christa's), 131
stickiness, 55, 57–60, 72–73, 96, 161
sticky numbers, 60
stories, 63, 161
strategies
    napkin, 127, 129–30, 138, 152, 163
    questioning, 123, 125–27, 130
structures
    belief, 37–42, 44, 161
    dump truck, 75–78, 80
    layered, 75, 78, 80–81

T

talk track, 3
temperature, 40–42
Tim (participant), 77
trust, 50–52, 153

V

value judgment, 133–35
Viola (participant), 158
voicemails, 70, 87, 132, 156
voice zoom, 65, 68–69
Voss, Chris, 144
    In *Never Split the Difference*, 144

W

waterboarding, verbal, 121
What Got You Here Won't Get You There
    (Goldsmith), 143
words
    concept, 60–63, 65, 72
    image, 60–63, 65, 72, 161
    signature, 102–4
workshop, 1–2, 5, 7, 43, 53, 132, 155

Made in United States
Orlando, FL
27 January 2023